STITCHING THE DARK

To Pat
with best wishes
Carole Satyamurti.

Carole Satyamurti is a poet and sociologist, who lives and works in London. She teaches at the Tavistock Clinic, where her principal academic interest is in the relevance of psychoanalytic ideas to an understanding of the stories people tell about themselves, whether in formal autobiography or in social encounters. She contributed to, and co-edited, with Hamish Canham, a collection of essays on the connections between poetry and psychoanalysis, *Acquainted with the Night: psychoanalysis and the poetic imagination* (Karnac, 2003).

Her poetry has been awarded several prizes. She won the National Poetry Competition in 1986, and received an Arts Council Writers' Award in 1988. In 2000, she received a Cholmondeley Award.

She is an experienced reader and workshop tutor, and teaches for the Arvon Foundation and for the Poetry School. With Gregory Warren Wilson, she runs poetry courses in Venice and Corfu, and has a particular interest in the links between poetry and visual art. She has been writer in residence at the University of Sussex, and a visitor in the Creative Writing Program at the College of Charleston, South Carolina.

Carole Satyamurti published three volumes of poetry with Oxford University Press, of which the first and third were Poetry Book Society Recommendations: *Broken Moon* (1987), *Changing the Subject* (1990) and *Striking Distance* (1994). Her fourth collection, *Love and Variations,* was published by Bloodaxe in 2000. Her latest book is *Stitching the Dark: New & Selected Poems* (Bloodaxe Books, 2005).

Carole Satyamurti

Stitching the Dark

NEW & SELECTED POEMS

BLOODAXE BOOKS

ISBN: 1 85224 692 8

First published 2005 by
Bloodaxe Books Ltd,
Highgreen,
Tarset,
Northumberland NE48 1RP.

www.bloodaxebooks.com
For further information about Bloodaxe titles
please visit our website or write to
the above address for a catalogue.

Bloodaxe Books Ltd acknowledges
the financial assistance of
Arts Council England, North East.

Cover printing by J. Thomson Colour Printers Ltd, Glasgow.

Printed in Great Britain by
Bell & Bain Limited, Glasgow, Scotland

to Martin

ACKNOWLEDGEMENTS

This book contains poems selected from previous collections. *Broken Moon* (1987), *Changing the Subject* (1990) and *Striking Distance* (1994) were published by Oxford University Press. *Love and Variations* (2000) was published by Bloodaxe Books.

Acknowledgements are due to the editors of the following publications, in which some of the new poems in *Stitching the Dark* first appeared: *Ambit, Chimera, Frogmore Papers, Illuminations, The Interpreter's House, Magma, Mslexia, Orbis, Oxford Magazine, Poetry London, Poetry Review, The Rialto* and *Thumbscrew*.

I would like to record my gratitude to the following people, all of whom read the new poems, and made valuable suggestions: David Black, Mimi Khalvati, Emma Satyamurti, Nancy Stepan and Martin Wilkinson. I owe special thanks to Gregory Warren Wilson, generous friend and ideal reader, who has commented on drafts of all these poems, with a truly rare perceptiveness.

CONTENTS

STITCHING THE DARK (2005)

13   *Personal Effects*
13   *Dear Departed*
14   *Shoes*
15   *Varanasi*
17   *Sathyaji*
18   Chesil Beach
20   Transatlantic
21   My Life as a Green-lipped Mussel
22   The Wood Turner of Jaubertie
24   Lessons in Air Kissing
25   Yellow
26   The Redness of Poetry
27   Waiting
28   The White Room
29   Reflections on Glass
30   Life Time
32   La Dame à la Licorne
33   Exposure
34   Facing Magritte
35   Woman Pursued by Dragon Flees into the Desert
36   Death of a Dancer
38   The Power of Prayer
39   *The Other Woman*
39   *The leaning tower of lemons*
39   *Brave face*
40   *Rough crossing*
41   *Sign*
41   *Reserve*
41   *Jealousy*
42   *Hands off*
43   *Life and death in another room*
43   *Out of range*
43   *Cancelling the deathbed scene*
45   The Silence of the Lions
46   The Arc de Triomphe Looks Defeated
47   Ankle Straps
48   On Not Going Anywhere
49   Lust in Translation
50   The Oldest Story
52   Cabaret Song
53   How I Altered History
54   Fable
55   At the Edge

56   Beauty's Not a Word They'd Needed Much
57   Community Care
58   Confidence
60   Immigrants
61   War Games
62   Playing with Words at Abu Ghraib
64   On the Map
65   Ballade
66   Give Me a Piece of Your Mind, Fat Man
67   Duende
68   Explaining Zero Sum from the Snowdrop Hotel

FROM **BROKEN MOON** (1987)
71   *Between the Lines*
75   Mouthfuls
76   My First Cup of Coffee
77   Erdywurble
78   Prognoses
79   Intensive Care
80   Getting There
81   Broken Moon
82   Mother's Girl
83   *From Rosa in São Martinho*
89   Women Walking
90   Day Trip
91   Curtains
92   Family Planning
93   Vertigo
94   Letter from Szechuan
95   Balancing Accounts
96   Poppies
97   The Uncertainty of the Poet
99   The Archbishop and the Cardinal
100   Pictograph in Dust
102   Going up the Line: Flanders
103   War Photographer
104   Graffiti

FROM **CHANGING THE SUBJECT** (1990)
106   Driving Through France
108   InterCity
109   On Not Being a Nature Poet
110   Strawberries
111   Showing
112   Birth Rite
113   Woman Bathing in a Stream: Rembrandt
114   The Balcony
115   Girls Awake, Asleep

116 Piccadilly Line
117 Christmas Circulars
118 *Changing the Subject*
128 Visiting Duncan
129 The Bed
130 Ruby Wedding
131 Partners
132 Reflections
133 Für Therese
134 Why I Lie in This Place
136 The Chairman's Birthday
138 Ghost Stations
140 Night Harvest

FROM **STRIKING DISTANCE** (1994)

143 This Morning
144 Waiting Room
145 The Fall
146 Passed On
147 Coat for an Undergraduate
148 File Past
149 You Make Your Bed
150 Skin Distance
151 Tide, Turning
152 Gifts
153 Woman in Brown
154 Presents for Duncan
155 Death Speaks After the Tone
156 The Way We Live Now
157 Where Are You?
158 Moment
159 Our Peacock
160 One
161 Out of Reach
162 Crossing the Border
164 Striking Distance
165 Advent in Bratislava, 1992
166 Thanatos
167 There Will Come a Time
168 The Trial of Lyman Atkins
169 America
171 *Sister Ship*
176 Turning Point
177 Cutting Loose
178 Life in Tall Houses
179 Il Conto
180 Tuesday at the Office
181 Wrong-footed

182 Blurred Vision
183 Ourstory
184 The Smell of Sweat

FROM **LOVE AND VARIATIONS** (2000)

186 Hands
187 My Wilderness
188 *Recorded Delivery*
192 *Boy with a Fish*
198 Leasehold
200 Les Autres *or* Mr Bleaney's Other Room
201 Leaving Present
202 The Woman Next Door
203 The Jew of Chantérac
204 Sunset Over Tottenham Hale
205 The Life and Life of Henrietta Lacks
206 The Front
207 Freedom of the City
208 Birthmark
209 The Blessing
210 Spring Offensive
211 Pentecost
212 By the Time You Read This
214 The Perversity of Mirrors
215 Missing You
216 Sitting for Manou
217 Two Quiet Women
218 Undine
219 Constanze's Wedding
220 It's Not the Same
221 Jacques Lacan's Table
222 Love and Variations

227 *Notes*

229 *Index of titles and first lines*

STITCHING THE DARK

(2005)

This stone, grey in air
glows deep red under water.
What colour is it?

Personal Effects

Dear Departed

Where are they now, the women you loved?
Eight of them sip Bordeaux, standing on your lawn
the day you are reduced to ashes, they to tears.

You loved women the way true explorers
loved Africa, moved by difference;
to find the source because it must be there.

Now, eyeing each other, they sift their words
and wonder what happened to the photographs:
Venus, Olympia, Origin of the World.

In each grey head, a girl unfolds herself
from tissue wrapping, relives Lake Naivasha, or the time
you made love thirty thousand feet above Dubrovnik:

lost girls, the ones who might have loved you differently;
who can't think for the life of them...when no one since
has made them feel so beautiful, or laugh so.

Shoes

Jackets are easy; even the dashing scarves,
Inverness cape with the red satin lining,
I bundle up for the Salvation Army,
for faceless other men. I can feel glad,
thinking these things will have an afterlife.

But these are one-man shoes
formed by your unconformable tread,
personal – impersonal as a death mask,
inviting me to slip inside; as if,
by standing in these good, creased husks,
my toes could reach yours.

How can I believe you won't need them now
or some time? Tonight, black winter;
rain's a frenzied tabla player beating on glass.
Aren't you walking barefoot out there,
your brahmin feet flinching
on the bitter, implacably hard ground;
wherever you are?

Varanasi

Would you have hated it
after a lifetime's flight from ritual –
this rigmarole of rice, curd, coconut,
gabbled Sanskrit you'd have spoken beautifully?

Mist muffled everything, Ganges, invisible,
and you in a steel canister inside a Tesco 'Bag for Life'.
Even the priest, who spoke no English, laughed.

Feeling my way down steep steps
to the waiting boat, entourage chattering alongside,
I wished it could be otherwise – not this *grand guignol*
but the two of us silent at the water's edge, reflecting
your wish to be scattered at the Manikarnika Ghat.

Then – suddenly there, fog-disembodied,
a man's head wrapped in orange cloth;
no pleated Sikh arrangement
but a rough swirl to ward off cold;
the fine face tranquil, motionless...gone.

Hours of chanting, the slap of oars
as we glided, a wraith-boat,
in customary sequence from ghat to ghat;
shock
as the river tugged you – ashes –
drenched in milk, ghee, prayers
out of my hands.

In a morning held in nets of nuanced grey,
deep orange was the only colour – that
and the tear-jerk pink of rose petals
eddying for a while, marking the place
where I let you go.

Orange headcloth, face, seem, in memory at least,
scarcely more substantial than you, now,
yet right – as I want to believe you were,
the point of this, after all, your homecoming,
your streaming out into the great Ganga
onward to the ocean and all the waters of the world.

I remember egrets perched on floating bamboo
on the filmy river. But I remember most
the orange turban, my mind returning to it
as birds to the bamboo –
somewhere to settle in perplexity.

A strip of cloth, a face...
I saw in them their quiddity and, if that,
then some truth of you might come
unstriven for – not so that you'd add up exactly,
not so I could say, *yes, you were That*,

but, emerging like that colour, from the fog,
something connecting me with you,
limitless, as the wide, white sky is;
timeless, as the consoling river is.

Sathyaji

(Lac Jemaye, France)

Dusk, and the boathouse keeper
calls the late, scattered boats
from beyond the curve
in the lake; calls them by name,
Hirondelle! Angelique! George Sand!
Are they real or imagined,
those smudges of black
in the shade of the far bank?
Again his call, carrying, returning.

What's in a name? You are —
in the name I called you by;
its weight and shape hard to convey
except — it lent itself to tenderness,
teasing and respect; closeness
and a certain distance.
Now it's a vessel
for the far-flung
only sure reality of you.

Love draws you back.
In saying your name, I see it
boat-shaped and luminous
stitching the dark,
returned from formless drift
about the world. Let me
recall you. I've words enough —
a sheaf of versions. My pen
engraves you differently each time.

Nothing can be held, or hurried.
Wind casts a shiver on the water;
shallows uncertain in withdrawing light.
A phalarope races its image
and is gone; reflected, relinquished,
discarnate as the distant boats
the boathouse keeper calls and calls,
only a name to summon each of them.

Yet, here they come.

Chesil Beach

Love is water, our shared history, stone;
each encounter alters us a little.

*

These limestone rocks
are records of the sea's wide journeys.
Rollers have pummelled them with glassy tons,
        or played tame, froth kissing their skins;
have brought them the world's particles,
        carried some away.

Stones get a taste of life like this;
and water daily meets its limitations.

Exchange,
        exchange;
                both are changed by it.

*

Each of us is water,
each is stone;
how difficult
to map those elements
in one another, truly.

*

A few mayfly decades can't comprehend
how long this shoreline has been trading
with the sea, in an alliance of opposites.

What constellation of improbabilities
has placed a trilobite or scrap of fern
inside some of these stoic rocks

as water, rhetorical and moody,
has lavished inexhaustible experience
in wearing stones into these shapes, these?

*

Now
and again
let's hold one another to the light
as if each were the one stone in the world,
as if there's no end to illumination.

*

Collectors, beady with desire,
raise their fossil hammers,
smash randomly
the smooth grey bellies of the stones
and, seeing mainly absence,

leave almost all,
inner worlds exposed
for the first time ever;
brown, grey, ochre chronicles
enlightening no one.

Who cares? Not stones.
As water sluices
round their splintered hearts,
with unimaginable slowness
they are becoming sand.

Transatlantic

Then, somewhere over Greenland, the sun
made jewels of ice crystals on the window,
thistledown on its way to space.

See them as a string of brilliants;
bright syllables, splitting memory
into its component bitter-sweets.

Or think of them as innumerable
light particles streaking from me to you
four thousand fibre optic miles

this instant; impulses, unbroken
but modulated now into sound –
my voice...this message...

My Life as a Green-lipped Mussel

If, by now, we have the faces we deserve
then read my lips – carefully rimmed
as though a watercolourist had skimmed

their outlines with a brushful of jade.
Jade for jealousy? For inexperience,
for not having got it right. The sense

of lips not opened recklessly enough
for fear of a capricious sea sealing
my mouth with sand; the feeling

that, beyond the distracting tides,
another life hungers to have been –
lived –
fertile, fluid, profligately green.

The Wood Turner of Jaubertie

(for Joel Beyney)

At the start of summer, as every year,
I visit the man who makes wooden fruits,
drawn by his house: the timbers chosen
for their slow arrival at that weight;
lime-wash stained ochre, pale terracotta –
pigments the walls needed to be reminded of.
Year by year, from a ruin,
without sell-short solutions,
he is giving the old house back to itself –

the garden too:
not the usual obedient French plot,
but a painter's palette of sweet peas,
poppies, campanula spilling along
curved stone paths; *potager* dense with promise
of pumpkins, haricots, the brilliant orange, yellow
and purple stripes of rare tomatoes.

And I'm drawn to the man himself.
He likes me to see these things,
to share his amazement,
for what's ordinary is joyful to him:
a crimson flowering quince, his whetted tools,
redstarts nesting in the box he made for them.

His craft is unexceptional:
bland apples, neat, symmetrical pears
though, like everything, they're meticulous,
carefully moulded copper stalks,
each calyx carved separately, stoppered in;
then the polishing with linseed oil and beeswax –
the type of object no one really needs, or loves,
but buys out of a vague restlessness.

This year, it's different. Weeping utterly
without embarrassment, he tells me
his nine-year-old died in June –
'aneurysm', he says (he'd never heard of it);
a secret fault that snatched her from him.

How could any words embody
the tread he never stops expecting, the flute lying silent?
How can my words of sympathy be more
than a clatter of small change thrown at catastrophe?
I wish I wasn't there.

He wants to tell me, though:
for months his work seemed pointless,
and dangerous – the tears, the spinning lathe.
But then his hands picked at the briar roots
he'd always scrapped till then and, needing to,
made an apple from the knotted ball.

He shows me – fruits heavier than before:
a blighted gourd, a fig, the lovely grain
wrenched and fissured to reveal
a world of corruption – the whole so compromised
it seems it must collapse, and yet the form holds.

A parallel. Of course – but that thought
doesn't honour the reach by hauled reach, the shift,
compelled by suffering, into terrain where craft
encounters art; finding a vessel for experience,
letting each root lay bare what it knows,
which he now shows me how to understand.

He sets a serious price for them
intending, I think, no one to buy them casually;
but to know that the time it takes
to bring these objects to completion,
and let them go, is a devotedness;
wanting us to see each piece as revelation
salvaged from the lip of what can be borne –
flawed and beautiful, an open question.

Lessons in Air Kissing

Among the other things
my mother didn't teach me
are that sex matters,
that work matters more,
how to quickstep the edge
between romance and self-respect

and any of the ways of becoming old:
sleazily, boastfully, resentfully,
as the plants grow...

or as a more and more
distant relation to one's self:
first, warm embraces,
then lips brushing skin,
cheek laid against cheek,
finally, kiss mockeries
mouthed, *mwah, mwah,*
into empty air.

Yellow

The way it stands against the dark,
rescuing brown from black, for instance.
The shapes the pen makes writing yellow.
The shapes the mouth makes saying *yellow,*
yellow – the way, even repeated, it resists inanity.

It's what stops the whole leafy, grassy world
being blue as the sky, and boring.

Of course there's jaundice, sulphur, fever, wasps,
but then – the vast swatch of natural pleasures:
the brimstone of butterflies, a blackbird's beak,
the heart of a marguerite, to be but arbitrary.

It's the colour of wealth – grain and honey,
saffron, amber, tiger's eye – and sharp, sad lemons.
How sinister and gorgeous are the words for it,
delicious on the tongue – gamboge, massicot,
xanthin, cadmium, luteolin.

In the next life, I'll have three yellow vases,
Qing, spirited from the Metropolitan Museum,
their different shapes singing to each other;

and, from the Top Kapi Palace, a small plain bowl
   most beautiful of all the Sultan's treasures
      deep, buttery perfection of its glaze
         soul of balance, lustre of joy
           Imperial Yellow.

The Redness of Poetry

At best, there's heart in it, and fire,
teeth and claws, willingness
to get its hands bloody;

there's debt, always, revolution
if you're brave; there are rags,
the very occasional letter day,

and thousands upon thousands of herrings.

Waiting

like a cat hunched before a cupboard,
hearing a faint rustle from inside;

like a cat whose stubborn need is solitude,
whose talent is devotion to detail;

whose habit is unreasoning belief,
being humble, and arrogant, by nature;

who asks no one's permission to be here,
now, doing nothing, and everything;

for whom the shapeless absence is a presence;
who seeks neither to stretch nor chivvy time;

whose imagining is one school of prayer,
profoundly still, intensely prepared

to seize what time must deliver to desire,
feeling already in the limbs, the ear,

the shape and voice of it; like a cat
who knows it draws every breath for this...

waiting.

The White Room

Longing for some thing to be different,
I gather it up, jagged with discontent,

carry it to the room of complete whiteness,
white so negative, so generous

it comprehends all colours; a domain
so still even the smallest shard of pain

falls away, relinquishing its hold
like a dead parasite. I take all I've railed

against, the ache of tiny consequence,
love lost, mistaken – and in that radiance

feel it dissolve, as simplifying fire
both cool and warm lets anger, fear, desire

merge with expanded light which, while it's there,
contains even the hardest facts there are.

Reflections on Glass

Mirrors should reflect a little before throwing back images
JEAN COCTEAU

Why are we drawn to glass?
Is it that such self-effacement gives us
all we need to know of paradox?
Duplicity: appearing solid;
disorderly in its internal life
as we are;
       our chaotic inner shifts,
our fragments, reflected back as coherent surface.
So we are doubly mirrored.

       *

Remember the afternoon when weather
slid through the window like a commentary
on itself – a documentary about clouds –
and on our shadow lives, so vivid and
beyond our power to change it, utterly?

       *

At Chartres, we puzzle over
a brilliant lexicon, transparent
to our illiterate ancestors. You'd think
our eyes, at least, see what theirs saw.
       But panes have flowed
downwards, imperceptibly, flow still,
refining faces, darkening hems of garments,
inviting us to reflect on illusion.

       *

Each day, there is a time when inside
and outside are provisional; when as light fades
what lies beyond the window is so balanced
with the interior you can scarcely tell reflection
from reality –
       and can choose to focus
on dusky sycamores, rooks homing,
or enter the frame and see your own face,
dispossessed, floating in the landscape.

Life Time

(for Hamish Canham)

Es ist der alte Bund
J.S. BACH,
Cantata BWV 106

Yours is the impossible story beyond all stories,
the journey whose end cannot be told by the traveller.
So few have spoken, even from the jetty
where you stand now. Fewer without bitterness.

Time is the narrative thread our joy calls for
and your plot ought to be a printer's error –
a novel we read again, wanting the end
to turn out differently, against all reason;

you're young – death too heavy to entertain.
We are atoms that fuse as miracles in time,
then fly apart: the bond, the covenant,
that links us all; the bind we must face alone.

The present – soon the past, once the future –
is the unique 'now', the vital instant
when we can practise freedom; and you do,
steadily, rich in insight. Even rarer

is your capacity for openness
that lets us – not share, for it's unshareable –
but see what you can lucidly face while yet
not tearing current happiness to shreds.

I'll die, but that is all I'll do for death.
Your living, so much on the side of life,
informed by truthfulness, is a state
where real thought marries heart and head.

I shall die. The future tense is knotted
into the weave and colours of our speech.
You have had to unravel layers of hope,
scaling down and down, until you catch

the specific gravity of those words – too dense
for language slanted at the usual angle.
Is there a veil between you and the old meanings?
Do you struggle to become bilingual?

Our lives are castles cancelled by the sea;
loss is the very grain of us. We keep
concentric bands braced around the self,
the mind's 'I' facing stubbornly away

from what must come: return to the oceanic
place that is no place, time without measure.
But your living and dying, the manner of it,
is taking root in us. It's like a fruit tree

planted in those you touch with love, and those
whom, nourished, they will touch. And it is clear
moral DNA, thread spinning out and out...
Dear friend, you were, you are, you will be – here.

La Dame à la Licorne

To say to the unicorn
oh beautiful
won't you come closer
crop the grasses
here in my field
for aren't we the same
blood and bone
I'll thread for you
a chain of stanzas
teach you your name

is to resist
its otherness
the mazy passages
of its heart
arrowed will
private scope
of its imagination
its awesome
aptitude for refusal;

is to lack thankfulness
for the here-today
taut flair of it
the grace
whose point is flight
as it swerves
leaping all ways
beyond reason
beyond sight.

Exposure

You wanted it over,
enduring stasis in the garden chair
posing to order
turning there…and there
hating, as ever,
that plyer of cheap trade, the camera,
though you're adept at parrying the stare
of focused lens or friend or lover,
finding directness hard to bear,
as if you fear
light could slip past your guard, discover
you as you really are.

You've taught me obliqueness –
how one can perceive
more by looking less;
and maybe an undeluded eye sees,
through its own faults, more than you believe;
but just as skewed perspective,
or flaws in a glazed pot, can bring alive
what otherwise would be dull dailiness,
so what I prize in you embraces
frailty of heart and mind. Think of this
when I'm not here to love
you as you really are, dear fugitive.

Facing Magritte

This painting proceeds like the drunkard's walk: reversible, and slow
to reach its destination – which I assume is to finish me, one way
or the other. Some days, he gives me marcel waves, say, or freckles,
then, when he's almost dared to let me please him, he takes pale indigo

and I lose my head. It's like dreaming, I imagine, or being fixed
just above blackout level, aware. My feet and legs were done,
for good I think, back in December, when snow-light made them
greenish. But the rest comes and goes – a week's work, perhaps,

then a moment's wash-out. He knows all about subjection –
but aren't we all subject (ha!) to other people's brush strokes?
Including him. Artists are such control fanatics. I get really
discouraged – it's hard to be so provisional. To know it, rather.

At least I have eyes, sometimes. But all these months, no arms.
What I'd do with them! Perhaps he's afraid of an accusing finger,
or stranglehold. Not the point. He creates me but he doesn't own
the way my skin hums, and he can't stop me rehearsing

the delicious moment when I'll feel sable shaping my right elbow.
Then I'll show him what pleasure there can be in imperfection!
I'll take the brush and palette from him – insist, if I have to –
and draw on all I've learned; begin to paint him in. Or out.

Woman Pursued by Dragon Flees into the Desert

She'd always loved the word
'immaculate', until they explained.
Even after Gabriel, it wasn't clear
this was a permanent commitment.
Not just a virgin but The Virgin.

The hydra-headed dragon
came to her door at night.
She smelled corruption on its breath
and pitied it, its skin scored
with self-loathing,
its terrible amour with death.

She looked it in the eyes, saw
herself: a tinselled effigy;
her Eternal Life sentence
a juggernaut of pain and terror.
She ran out of the town,
into the clean silence of the desert.

How many desperate decades of the rosary
reeled backwards to her then;
countless pleas for intercession.
She saw she was to star
in a two-thousand year long tragedy,
a non-speaking part.

That timeless trap, the allure
of making all the difference;
and though the khamsin whispered
tears...miracles...make nothing happen,
she stopped running. Across the sand
the creature crawled to drag her into history.

Death of a Dancer

Hours later, it seems, the pigeons are still wheeling
around the cluttered domes of the cathedral,
great drifts of them, unsettled by the utterly no further
smack of flesh on the hard slabs of the piazza.

We stare, stupidly aware of our place in the aesthetic
mise en scène, the way we've been cast as witnesses.
Though he's a stranger to us, perhaps we feel, a little,
that it was we who left such desperation uncontained?

This was the most free act, his sufficient and empty
farewell performance, executed to perfection,
the note in his breast pocket, his own review – although,
falling, might he have wished it could last

longer, be a slower sequence so, for a while,
he could take death in his arms, airborne
in the most eloquent of tangos, letting the music
resolve around his final plunge to earth?

Since we've all known what it is to lack consolation,
but how the pain silts over in the end, we want him
to unfold from the crumple of blood and splinters
(less than you'd expect) to hang head down in air

then rise, toes pointed, limbs spreadeagled,
up the great height of the campanile – as if the gods
were fishing, and he the precious catch being lifted
on an invisible, unbreakable line – and now

to back-flip over the barricade and stand
cruciform, shouting *!understands one No.*
You could think he is about to prophesy, but he droops
his head, backs towards the stairwell, climbs,

ladderwise, down to the sun-bleached square,
withdraws, contrapposto, past the unseeing queues.
We can imagine him on the vaporetto retreating
up the Grand Canal, the reversing bus, the clinic

where they suck back soft words and sweeteners,
flick glances from the clock. And he: *.invented have I*
figures the dance can one No .tanguero greatest
world's the am I' It isn't like that, of course.

We were a kind of company. But he couldn't choreograph
the way our minds slide now towards prosecco.
Or how the pigeons move on their own flight paths,
innocent of sorrow, free without knowing it.

The Power of Prayer

She read about the grape diet,
how the author had cured himself
by eating nothing but.

She couldn't afford grapes;
it came to her – grapefruit
was almost the same,

better even, more explicit.
By eating the flesh she could eat
the word, almost. *Repair-gut.*

All metaphor was out;
the point was the thing itself
and the word for it.

In another time and place
she would have been beatified.
As it was, people were appalled

at such pitilessness, though never
knowing whether the tumour shrank
before she died of malnutrition.

The Other Woman

The leaning tower of lemons

After he's gone
and the week
settles into silence
hedged by his breath
she sees
no trace of him
in the blandness
of blue cotton
mournful catechism
of bowl and spoon
but in a corner
finds
standing
on one another's
shoulders
lemons
extraordinary
as Chinese acrobats
balancing.

Brave face

It's all in the seeing,
the half full / half empty
moment by moment
way of being.

It's in the not saying,
not lifting the lid
of the can; the choice
between smiling and crying.

It's in winging, singing
C major, when what's
in her mind is D minor;
it's in not clinging.

This sequence is loosely based on the difficult relationship between Gwen John and Rodin

It's in willed delight –
as now, when they're taking
the long way round
for the sake of a sight

of a throng of jonquils,
the simplicity
of an everyday treat,
fandango of daffodils.

Aren't they marvellous!
He stares through the railings.
It's dusk. November.
Yes, she says, *fabulous!*

Rough crossing

They're not touching
and Not Talking
not like lovers anyway
which they haven't been for a while;
she thinks, maybe they're ex-lovers
only he hasn't advised her of the fact.

So she says...
and he says nothing.
So she says... (which, if she'd been herself
she'd have had the sense not to).
And he says, *You're just like all the others.*
And she (who'd taken pride in not being,
but quite a star in the self-denying love department)
screams:

Oh, you've noticed!
I'm Baba Yaga with blood-scarlet eyes;
I'm the shot-gun type who expects you to deliver;
I'm the Belle Dame, I plan to suck you
wan as moonlight;
I'm Venus Flytrap, vagina dentata...

No she doesn't.

The old safe-ish script scrolls from her mouth
like ticker-tape at a port;
and the words are speaking her,
they're pennants, nailed to the mast
of their just-about seaworthy craft.

Sign

Even the day
when the hurt they give each other
renders them brittle as dead leaves,
and as separate,

a word arriving on their lips
at the same moment
affirms them – as happens often
but is unlooked-for now.

It's as if a hidden watercourse
had blessed them, bubbling
briefly up into the light;
or as if a goldfinch

had darted down to take a grain
from each of them; a split
second of all the difference
brushing his hand and hers.

Reserve

She gives him – things. They're paradoxical,
her and not-her, part of that part of her
he can accept; and she takes such pleasure
in finding them they're hardly gifts at all.

He can't take what she most wants to give.
She lays it down in her mind's cellarage
not knowing if it will improve with time,
be dignified by dust, vintage love.

But she knows – when she doesn't write or call,
doesn't ask when asking seems natural,
blocks from her tongue what's longing to be said –
that silence is the dearest gift of all.

Jealousy

Interminable nights
when street lamps turn the room
ashy sick and senseless and

a picture show loops for hours
so dull; so terrible she can't stop looking.
She distracts the projectionist with tea and pills

but here it comes again, the bed scene
where his slow, loving hands – it's that –
strike her every, every time;

while on the wall, rare ikat silk –
her last foolish birthday present – bleeds,
glows like the blessing it surely must become.

Hands off

She'll try to be the just good friend
with both hands tied. Easy.
She's free-wheeling down hill.

Hands are prone to stickiness;
they ask, reach out, grasp;
hands write queasy letters.

Hands ring his door-bell,
ache in freezing weather,
above all, open things up.

This way, she's a circus horse,
blinkered, balancing
to a Viennese waltz.

Not that it's an act –
it's real enough,
just a bit Für Elise-y,

when she used to risk
Fantaisie Impromptu.
It's slightly uneasy

smiled greetings; simple
as alliteration, as rhymes
jingling in the breeze –

Look, no hands.

Life and death in another room

In her dream, she doesn't know who
has stabbed him between the ribs.
She scrunches her blouse into a wad,
presses it against his side

but he's draining his heart out
into her bed, an intimacy
much too late. Blood
pumps and pumps.

In this life, her bed is empty
even of imagining him.
In the other one, he stains her
indelibly – not now from a wound,

but from a split across his belly
which is round as the world,
the flesh inside porous
like pumice; like bread.

Out of range

She counts the years and months it went on before they parted
and she's consoled, until she sees it never started.

Cancelling the deathbed scene

He asks her to promise she'd let him know if she were dying,
        and she promises,
touched, but a bit embarrassed for him, suspecting he has no idea
        of the enormity;
and wonders if he's thinking of an Act III dénouement, a moment when
        he'll discover feeling –
and words for it he's never found before. She could tell him they'd be
        invalid in that last dance salon,
foil-wrapped chocolate money, risking nothing, incapable of standing
        as tender
for anything beyond themselves, anything muscular or durable;
        the currency of love
(hers spend-like-water prodigal, his eked prudently) debased
        to moonshine.

43

And after all – when her living couldn't reach him, all her flighted energy
    in words, and otherwise,
her rash speculation with new minted meaning that left her broke, so that
    she has come to the very brink
of despair with language itself, art itself, so that she is empty and anodyne;
    when he has shown her
in so many bitter ways how far he couldn't take her; when she has wasted
    herself right down to zeros,

then, why would she offer him her dying – her last, most high-denomination
    note, lesser ones
having faded, times without number, unwelcome as flowers he won't
    allow into the house?
Why would she – but for the never-say-die, hard habit of loving him,
    the final, unvoiced, settling for this?

The Silence of the Lions

All the savannah-sultry afternoon
the tannoy van intrudes on every space,
every alley, every shaded room
in Bernay, announcing the performance
...*grand cirque, à six heures* on the waste ground.
A gypsy lion tamer's the big draw.

The older citizens of Bernay draw
their blinds a little lower, the afternoon
reserved for sleep; they dream of the playground
they knew as children, before time and space
were cages, before the habit of performance
confined their dreaming to a tidy room.

Out on the jostling streets, there's hardly room
for all the children the loudspeakers draw
into the market square. A performance
is rare in Bernay, and this afternoon
there's a preview — two lions cram the space
of a battered cage on wheels, a dish of ground

beef beside them. If only they ground
their teeth, or roared, they'd open up a room
in the imagination. There'd be space
for rage; they'd be like lions children draw
to scare themselves. But they sleep all afternoon,
already tamed, ahead of the performance.

Or is oblivion a mere performance?
Might they be thinking of a hunting ground —
feasts of impala, drowsy afternoons
under a thorn tree — where a lion has room
to be a lion, defend his pride, can draw
luxurious breath, king of boundless space?

The children know about too little space.
They've begun to get the measure of performance,
of exile from themselves. They'd like to draw
courage from a lion who stands his ground
and won't be tamed, won't settle for a room
defined by wire mesh. But this afternoon

there's no space for rebellion. At the waste ground,
countdown to performance. From room to room
children draw lessons from the afternoon.

The Arc de Triomphe Looks Defeated

(Paris, 2003)

This is the world's third hottest place;
only Seville and Dubai are more infernal.
It's as if our bones have turned pliable
like skate – no real bones at all
but a framework for flapping, through water
no more resistant than this viscid air.

Whether to get up from the café table
has become a calculus of effort.
The heat is visible, a dusty syrup
we wear as second skin. My silver
jewellery has turned soot black.
Time slumps.

It's the dying that's easy – the elderly,
in too many thousands for the mortuaries,
overflow into Norbert Dentressangle's
refrigerated lorries, parked under guard
in *zones industrielles* until their families
come back from holiday, or don't.

The social patchwork's cracking, loosening.
The mad are madder – we're all a bit insane,
normal restraint liquefying into love
or fury. A man hurls bottles at the bar
of Amélie's café. A vagrant strips;
someone turns a hosepipe on him.

Along the rue Duhesme, knickers, parted
from their most intimate skin, are strewn
at intervals, like abandoned babies
whose mothers are better off without them.
The Eiffel tower dives into the Seine.
Mona Lisa bares her teeth.

Ankle Straps

You'd imagined it as a virgin thinks of sex;
like gliding on ice in sweeping figures,
your feet tingling with the gift of tongues –

lapiz, giro, salida: names dizzy
with a vision of lift-off, flight
curved by the rhythms of the South.

But it's the old mortal story – sweat, soreness,
terrible timing; the ways you've always
struggled to understand, to be understood,

subject to the same misreadings;
your feet, no good at languages, faltering
against his, as you fail to follow, again.

No shame quite like it since the time
you couldn't get the hang of three-point turns
and backed into Mr Telford's greenhouse –

though now and then, suddenly, you get it,
and you are sublime, fluent, subtle,
weight offered and received exactly right.

So you keep on keeping on; and so does he;
dancing *ochos, sacadas* to the great Piazzolla
like stars from Buenos Aires; in your dreams.

On Not Going Anywhere

Dearest, what do you mean?

The river flows continually to the sea.
But ask, 'Where is the river?'
and you will always find it
there, on the far side of the trees.

Where did the sun go when it set?
Did it drop down to Australia
to rouse the kookaburra? No,
the sun doesn't go anywhere. Like us.

Perhaps you mean it's not going
to the Registry Office, the Nationwide,
the ante-natal class. There, I agree with you.
But neither is it going to the wall, the dogs...

It's true, we haven't turned
into Venetian carnival, or a pair of Arab
race-horses, or a portmanteau brimming
with Kanchipuram silk

but aren't the best places unspeakable?
Uncharted openings between names?
Darling, we are anywhere already.
Anywhere is where we are.

Lust in Translation

When the International Language Crimes Tribunal
has considered *Collateral Damage* and *Friendly Fire*
they might turn to *Love*. Love and the French.
Love and French films in particular – the verve and sanity
they drain from the most important word there is.

It's the moping and mooning they do, those lovers,
at the traffic, into the mirror and out of it,
the way they're in love with themselves in love with
themselves... Where is fun, real adversity, ordinary luck?
What about the grit, and the time, the sheer *time* love takes?

Love may make you smile. It makes them desolate:
je t'aime (glycerine glazing flawless cheeks); *je t'aime*
(achingly chic cardigan pulled around skeletal shoulders
since, whatever else, 'love' ruins appetite) as though
to utter it brings them eyeball to eyeball with *le néant*.

O love distilled to the mating dance of moths!
They're children in a chocolate shop, tearing off
the wrappings. *Je t'aime*, they pant, between mouthfuls;
or even *je vous aime* since, often, they've met so recently
they're not even on *tutoying* terms.

In fact they should come clean and go intransitive:
J'aime, they should say, *je désire immodérément*,
to describe a condition like hayfever or a craving
for celeriac: something seasonal and a yawn, except
to fellow sufferers. *Je t'aime* – it's almost a nervous tic

but you'd better believe it, at least a little, because,
otherwise, the whole film collapses like wet meringue.
So you almost manage to put yourself in her place, or in his,
except that what they need, you realise, is animation –
soul, and muscle, and a hell of a lot more speed;

and 'what was all that *about*?' we say, as we stumble
out of one more ill-spent evening. 'Love.' Of course.
But surely we missed some irony, a hint of the sublime –
we who won't recall this story of 'love' from a dozen others;
we who don't know the meaning of the word, apparently.

The Oldest Story

Gender gap

Adam said to Eve, a bit down-hearted,
'Why do we have to *talk*, can't you leave
well alone? Don't shake the bloody branch!'
The first star-crossed millennium had started.

In praise of mathematics

I'm ready to believe
numbers are beautiful as speech,
eloquent as words.

Trouble is, there are so few
numerate pebbles on the beach,
and they are nerds.

The less loving one

Auden said it first:
when you no longer treasure
their every word; when you hear a groan
and realise it's the heart (your own)
you'd thought was durable as gutta percha –
that's the worst.

Squib

When they invented fireworks
did it strike them
that the lit fuse
excitement mounting
the fizz, gee-whizz
bang and shriek
of flying stars
soft explosions
cascades of colour
ooh and aah
transformation of
dull rods into marvels

are so much more
like the real thing
than the real thing:
groan and shudder
little spurt
limp
damp
squib?

Cabaret Song

I'm brilliant at clearing my cupboards of clutter,
    at seeing what will and won't do.
When it comes to the boot I'm the grande dame of Oxfam,
    but not when it comes to you.

I don't mind a row – don't care when, don't care how –
    I'm a fishwife, virago, a shrew.
I'm known for the tough line I take with jerks – but I'm
    a wimp when it comes to you.

When dancing the tango, I let every man go –
    I'd never request a reprise;
but, though I lose face, when I'm in your embrace
    I say 'Let's have *one* more dance please, please, please!'

I am La Guillotine when I'm drafting a line
    letting metre and rhyme have their due.
Inversions and adverbs I really can't bear,
I censor cerulean, never say ne'er,
I can 'murder my darlings' and not turn a hair –
    but damn it! not you, not you.

How I Altered History

Wild splashing – a lizard
fallen in the rainwater bucket
was scrabbling at the smooth sides

frantic to be out,
delicate fingers not up to it,
flanks fighting for breath.

It's a privilege to save a life;
some people never do.
And since life is life, indifferent

to worth or benefit, it was as though
I'd saved Mahatma Gandhi, Shelley,
Barthes – or any joker

whom attentiveness and a well-placed hand
could have turned from premature extinction.
As it was, it was a lizard with no tail

I tipped, ungrateful beast,
urgent for ants, twitching for a quarrel,
into the rest of its singular career.

Fable

Two dogs are fighting for your heart
    Child, my little one.
One must win and one must depart
    Granddaughter of mine.

One of them growls; he's violent, greedy
    Child, my little one.
His face is gaunt and he's full of envy
    Granddaughter of mine.

The other is gentle, his eyes are warm
    Child, my little one.
He wishes no one the slightest harm
    Granddaughter of mine.

Which dog will win the fight for my heart
    Old grey-headed one?
Which will win and which will depart
    Grandfather of mine?

The fight is a close-run fight indeed
    Child, my little one,
And the dog who will win is the one you feed,
    Granddaughter of mine.

At the Edge

This could be the still centre
in the hurtle of travel.
You, stranger, opposite,
wearing yourself like perspex,
seeming visible,
glances glancing off you
to die on the floor –

Look at me.

This is the visual turn
when looks can become things
and things can kill –
sane people know that.
Let's chance a nakedness
beside which 'love' is safe
hide and seek, noisy blind convention.

I want to look at you

even though each strung nerve
is crazy for escape,
even though eyes don't do this,
don't meet without reserve
in a giddy recession of mirrors,
at once entering, being entered,
meta-physical.

We bring nothing, can lose nothing

yet I sweat terror –
that in-sight so personal,
so abstract, might bring us to
an unimagined
chute into infinity.

Look – let me – look, stranger,
I to eye to I to

Beauty's Not a Word They'd Needed Much

For weeks he worked to clear his ground; neighbours would glance
across at him piling up rubble, hardcore. *Public nuisance,*

all that mess, they said, *what's wrong with turf, maybe paving,*
containers for colour, like the rest of us? They couldn't stop looking

though it was a sort of aggravation. Every daylight hour he stood
out there; often he'd just stare, then pace the land, dig, spread

soil from bags. He built a glasshouse. Soon, trays fuzzed with green,
and when May came he planted – spindly seedlings; sparse, mean,

but slowly a picturebook of leaves opened across the black,
and later such flowers came they found the word 'miraculous' –

the way the beds embroidered themselves, how a run of water
brought stones alive; everything more than itself for being together.

For all of two minutes they thought *we could do that, get hold*
*of books, memorise the names…*but knew they couldn't match his bold

idea of possibility, the way he'd waited. He had the patience
to allow plants to become themselves; they didn't have his confidence –

that was it. What wealth he must have had inside, to see
the whole; mind's-eye glory lighting up his winter, while they…

Maybe if he'd got them to help, shown them how. Or if he'd built
a fence. His kind of thing felt out of place. Almost an insult.

He was out one afternoon; there was high laughter on the street,
a party-time excitement as the kids went in and trashed it,

trampled beds, hacked trellises, smashed the flowering dogwood,
the glasshouse. The neighbours didn't stop them. They understood.

Community Care

'I haven't seen you, love.' She means it kindly,
the night cleaner on the tube, knowing
it's cold enough to freeze your bollocks off.
It's not the Hilton, but it isn't snowing
down here. And there's the mice for company.

I haven't seen you. No one ever did –
mother a druggie, seven foster carers;
they tried, but found him unapproachable.
Always kicked out for 'challenging behaviour'.
Homeless now, and still only a kid.

What the mice suggested to him then,
what sooty invitation, who can say?
Perhaps he felt he wasn't really there.
Commuters were told, 'incident... delay'.
They grumbled, but most got to work by ten.

No name on him. Five quid, and a spent
cigarette lighter. Spent was how he looked.
The cleaner lost her job. No one claimed him.
Eventually, a funeral was booked
at Hendon Crem. Only the cleaner went.

Confidence

A good lie's an achievement, like tightrope walking.
Choose your mark. Hold your nerve, look well ahead.
It's a matter of tone, judging how much to spell out,
what can be left to willingness.

My mum's died – I've got to get to Brighton.
Tears pour down her face. She's very thin.
I think, there must be a whole history
behind this, accosting a stranger. For me

the choice is simple: believe her –
probably be conned; or don't – never know.
I give her money. Next day, she's back,
promises she'll repay, but now she must have

cash for the undertaker, for phone calls
to uncles in Canada. Next morning, another
plausible crisis; the story blossoms. I listen;
and I give, colluding, testing her.

Every lie, or poem, is autobiographical.
The facts may be untrue, but in the telling
and the choice of elements, another truth
seeps round the margins of the frame;

so when I start to have a sense of spectacle,
a feeling that she's in this with me, watching
the plot unfold – and that's the point for both of us –
the ground shifts. I say No.

She goes pale with shock; without a word
she turns and runs down the path. Then I realise
this was violence: I've smashed the whole, frail,
necessary house of stories, trampled the truth of it –

since someone who says she's lost her mum
certainly has, one way or another.
Of course, there was the money, she needed that
(drugs, I heard afterwards – she was known),

but as important, surely, was her creation
brick by virtual brick, of meaning, entitlement,
the start of something; a listener who made it possible.
And now she's back on the empty streets of herself.

We both know about shaping truth to secret purposes.
If I had met her, risk for risk, perhaps she'd not
have left the message later, a pathetic threat
from a public phone. Anonymous.

Immigrants

All those names mangled on Ellis Island.
Or they themselves, after so many days,
sighting Liberty, Mother of Exiles,

stood at the ship's rail, and felt their name,
closer than skin before, might not sit well
on the new citizen they would become

and with a pen, performed quick surgery:
cut, stitched, and were remade as Mann,
Peterson, Linden, Carpenter or Leary;

while englished colours lined up on the deck
to stream out to the cities of America –
Silver, Gold, Green, Rose, Black.

Others, more secretive or radical,
made up new names – as if the entirely new
were possible, as if each syllable

didn't carry its hidden freight of need
and passion, every choice betray its roots
in loss, to those who knew how to read;

and to convince themselves, silently
rehearsed the strange names, until they were
garments they could believe would fit one day,

each repetition fleshing out a dream
of plenitude, romance, detaching them
from the more visceral richnesses of home.

That arrival must have been the last
swung moment, out of time. Between.
No language now, or ever, for the vast

weightlessness of life about to happen.
Only the shouldering of a name too small
for all they longed for. And the dock gates open.

War Games

Peace-keeping's for pansies. This is Last of the Mohicans stuff.
(U.S. Marine preparing for the assault on Baghdad)

You've put on war paint – dark green stripes
and patches: cover, disguising and distinguishing.

Perhaps you did it years ago, at children's sleepovers,
Indian brave faces. These same touching haircuts, probably.

It isn't like we war-gamed it. No, it's the real war story:
terror, terrible confusion; the poor pitched against the poorer,

not understanding, in the daze of noise and sleeplessness,
what it's all for, though you think you knew, once,

when you hadn't imagined the way they'd hate you,
hadn't pictured the vast indifference of the land.

Chances are, you'll never again find the words to tell it
so it comes out simple, as it was before you fired at children.

America has been your fact of life. But you're descended
from adventurers, the dispossessed, the world's dissenters,

and it could have been you, ignorant of English like these
crushed losers with no face-paint to hide their fear.

Playing with Words at Abu Ghraib

1

Call it hazing
     that makes it a prank
Call it letting off steam
     it's understandable
Call it softening them up
     that makes it a duty
Call it stressing them out
     that's psychology
Call it interrogation
     that's expertise
Call it a few bad apples
     the rot stops there.

Call it torture
     it's only abuse
Call it violation
     stuff happens
Call it contravention
     it's 'legally available'
Call it corrupt
     it's military necessity
Call it a war crime
     they're non-legal combatants
Call it wrong
     trust us, trust us.

2

Shoes, bodies, piled up without shame
but even at Auschwitz-Birkenau the guards
taking photographs for souvenirs
didn't put themselves in the frame.

Here we have Sabrina from Tallahassee
majorette smile, perfect teeth
thumbs up beside the bashed up
shrink-wrapped Manadel al-Jamadi.

Here we have Charles and Ed
with Lynndie grinning, posing
feet planted like one of the boys
with her prisoner on a lead.

This is payback, carnival
when anything's allowed and, hey,
there are words for it.
Who says? The General.

   3

This is Lynndie
This is Chip
Lynndie likes fun
Chip likes fun

This is Ali
Is Ali a dog?
No Ali is not a dog
Ali is a man

Lynndie plays with Ali
Chip plays with Ali
This is fun says Lynndie
This is fun says Chip
I like fun says Lynndie
I like fun says Chip
Ali does not like fun

Lynndie and Chip are having fun
Jump Ali jump says Lynndie
Sing Ali sing says Chip
This is fun says Lynndie
This is fun says Chip

Fuck Ali says Lynndie
Take a picture says Chip
We like fun say Lynndie and Chip
Smile says Lynndie
Fun fun fun fun fun says Chip.

On the Map

...the motorway starts here – the thick red line
between Watling and Minton Parva;

and for once you'll be in at the beginning
not filtering in as if you hadn't quite the right to

join a going concern. It'll be a clear departure
when often you don't see how you came to be here.

But cruising down the slip road, you find
others are already there, again, careering by

barely allowing you in; understanding something
you don't – a tip-off, a newer map perhaps –

smug at having started from somewhere
definite, together; and you have no way

of knowing the place they left from, the point
they'll return to; where the main road really begins.

Ballade

This winter morning, driving north,
I like it that no one knows where
I am – or if I am. It's worth
the risk to feel this padded chair
streaking like gunshot from nowhere
to nowhere; to pretend that space
is infinite, that I can tear
through the screen of time and place.

The motorway's heat-shivered path
extends to vanishing, and there's
no other car in sight. The earth
is stripped of life, the lanes a pair
of virtual highways; now I stare
into a screen-game where I race
solely against myself, career
through the screen of time and place

into the afterlife, where death
deals me what I deserve; yes, there
is highway everlasting – birth
process without delivrance – fair
sentence for one inclined to sneer
at people who don't want to face
solitude, who refuse to peer
through the screen of time and place.

ENVOI

Travel like me – unless you fear
the headlong flight, the reckless chase
into the wordless, silvered air
through the screen of time and place.

Give Me a Piece of Your Mind, Fat Man

I want to feel my bones packed snug in their upholstery,
for my whole poundage to shake with seismic laughter. Let me
be a surprise, as you are, mesmerising with your deep voice
and your high voice, when people expect you to be a joke.

Show me how warm it is when small children and cats snuggle
in the mounds and folds that spread from north to south of you.
Teach me to sing out of the ampleness of my fat cheeks, massive chest,
my glorious acoustic; to be a hero in the face of tittering.

Let my sex astonish people, since they hadn't reckoned on it.
Let me give orders without apologetic fidgeting. I want to know
your dolphin buoyancy in water, your understated footwork
on the dance floor, axle in a whirling dazzle of jive.

I'd hate to have to act impervious in restaurants, eat in the face
of all those mimsy appetites staring as though you had the pox,
sucked-lemon faces glad they won't have your coronary.
But when you take off your clothes and strut in a sash,

wrestle, huge weight balancing huge weight – I'd like to feel that.
I want to be given a second firing, to be lifted newly from the kiln
generous as a great bellied pot. Corpulent and wise Gautama,
give me your staying power, your gravity, your far-seeing smile.

Duende

That great operatic bunch of tulips you bought on impulse
filled my arms with scarlet blooms already at their best,
stiff-stemmed, glossy, only a ghost of fade about them.

Days after, they were flourishing on borrowed time,
on show in satin flounces; flurry of flamenco dancers,
the increasing torsion of their scrinchy leaves,

their proudly turned heads, refusing to collapse.
It's a week now. Water in the cool yellow vase
is murky with decay, and the tulips are no longer

drawing on reserves. Past all pretence at integration,
their petals are curled rags, hurt colours.
They're entering a change of state, papery flames

writhing in silent desolation. But last week's flowers,
so bright, so upsprung, were no more essential
than these tattered queens with so much death in them.

Explaining Zero Sum from the Snowdrop Hotel

We have blind spots.
Five times at least I've asked you to explain parallax;
you say 'zero sum' is meaningless to you.

High in the Alps, I've held out for this room
against Americans whose sleep, now, will toss uneasily
through the trundle of lorries – the main road;
beyond it, trains clanking in from Italy.
My gain = their loss; that's zero sum.

My window overhangs a stream, high on meltwater,
whirling past under an agate sky. At evening,
an invisible blackbird pitches his notes clear
across, until the song seems to draw
its phrases from the river's rush and welter.

If, with each new tune, the water lost energy,
became less abundant until it thinned to a trickle
while the blackbird voiced ever more opulent
torrents of sound – that would be zero sum.

Or if, by its acrobatics, by sheer verve, the river
so daunted and engulfed the bird's inventions
that his song became mere cheep and whistle –
that would be zero sum.

But the blackbird opens his throat, his song
bubbles and chuckles with all the river that is in it;
and the music returns to the water such vibrations
that the river becomes infused by song,
embodying, in endless tumble to the sea,
that sound, and its own.

This is not zero sum – this is gain and gain.

from

BROKEN MOON

(1987)

Between the Lines

1

Words were dust-sheets, blinds.
People dying randomly, for 'want of breath',
shadowed my bed-times.
Babies happened;
adults buried questions under bushes.

Nouns would have been too robust
for body-parts; they were
curt, homeless prepositions – 'inside',
'down there', 'behind', 'below'. No word
for what went on in darkness, overheard.

Underground, straining for language
that would let me out, I pressed to the radio,
read forbidden books. And once
visited Mr Cole. His seventeen budgerigars
praised God continually.

He loved all words, he said, though he used
few to force a kiss. All that summer
I longed to ask my mother, starved myself,
prayed, imagined skirts were getting tight,
hoped jumping down ten stairs would put it right.

My parents fought in other rooms,
their tight-lipped murmuring muffled
by flock wallpaper.
What was wrong, what they had to say
couldn't be shared with me.

He crossed the threshold in a wordless
slam of doors. 'Gone to live near work,'
my mother said, before she tracked down
my diary, broke the lock, made me cut out
pages that guessed what silence was about.

2

Summer, light at five. I wake, cold,
steal up the attic stairs,
ease myself into Mrs Dowden's bed,
her mumble settling to snores again.

In a tumbler, teeth enlarged by water;
her profile worrying, a shrunken mask.
Her body's warm, though,
smells of soap and raisins.

I burrow in her arm's deep flesh
forgetting, comforted. Finding out
with fingers that creep like stains
that nipples can be hard as pencil ends,

breasts spongy, vaster than a hand's span;
and further down under the nightdress,
a coarseness, an absence;
not what I'd imagined.

3

Chum Larner, Old Contemptible,
badge on his lapel, barbered our hedges
for parade; nipped capers off nasturtiums,
their peppery juice evoking India,
the dysentery that wiped out his platoon,
'But yer can't kill orf a Cockney sparrer!'
His epic stories rattled gunshot,
showed me what dying meant.

The shed – tropical dusk, air thickened
by tarred twine, drying rosemary,
his onion sandwiches. Sitting on his knee
I'd shiver as he told about the ghost
of Major Armstrong's fancy woman
who wandered the cantonment, crooning.
My mother stopped me going,
suspecting him, perhaps, of more than stories.

4

Upstairs was church,
a clock ticking somewhere
and my mother, a penitent,
breasting the stairs,
smile upside-down,
streak of tears
gone when I looked again.

No sound behind the door
I dawdled past on tiptoe,
where strangers were allowed

and where, wanting more than breath,
my grandmother was being dulled
by blue walls, too much sleep,
the brownish, disinfected smell;
by being too delicate to touch,
by no one singing to her,
by hunger, chafing her to bone.

5

'...someone for you to play with.'
But I could tell she'd be
useless at throwing, or bricks,
no good at pretending.

'Isn't she sweet?' Couldn't they see
she was yellow, creased, spotty,
an unfinished frog, a leaky
croaky cry-for-nothing?

'Be gentle now!' But I was
doing what they said, playing.
My best doll's bonnet
fitted her floppy beetroot head.

She smelled of powdered egg.
They warmed her vests.
She slept against my mother's skin.
'How do you like her?' Send her back.

6

Books let me move close to them,
breathe their scent of secret places.
They broke through net curtains,
stained glass, tea-time
and dared to shout, take risks
for love or principle.
One was an unsuitable companion,
revealed with disappointing diagrams
the body's terra incognita.

People were difficult to read,
foreign, with uncut pages.
I could see their spines braced
to support the weight of hidden words.
Their covers carried all the information
they thought necessary.

In my dream, I always woke
just as I reached to touch
the most beautiful, the only book
that would have shown me everything.

7

Did I know what I'd find?
I see myself
sneaking, because I must,
across her rose carpet;
turned cat, criminal
without the nerve.

I'm sliding open
the middle drawer –
the letters, wrong
in this habitat of hair-grips,
powder leaves,
the smell of evening gloves.

I can still see
his love-shaped writing,
ink confidently black,
vowels generous
as mouths, fluent
underlined endearments.

And my father's
pinched hieroglyphics,
clipped sentences
the shape of pain
trying to be dignified.
Words pulled out by the root.

Has hindsight twisted it?
I remember no surprise,
only the lurch of knowing
here was the edge
of something absurd,
a terminal complexity.

Mouthfuls

They lasted longer then.
Mars Bar paper crackled
as we rewrapped half for later,
sliced the rest
to thin cross-sections,
arranged them like wedding-cake –
loaves and fishes.

Sherbet lemons, hard against the palate,
vicious yellow. Strong sucking
made them spurt, fizz, foam,
sugar splinters lacerate
the inside of my cheeks,
surprising as ice crystals in the wind
that cut my legs through socks.

Licorice comfits shaken in a tin
made marching music.
Or they were fairy food –
each colour wrought a different magic:
mauve for shrinking,
green, the power to fly,
red, the brightest, eternal sleep.

The oddity of gob-stoppers:
tonguing each detail
of the surface – porcelain,
tiny roughnesses,
licking, rolling it, recapturing
the grain and silk of nipple;
rainbows glimpsed only in mirrors.

A shorter life for jelly babies –
drafted into armies, black ones last,
or wrapped in paper shawls in matchbox beds,
taken out, chewed from the feet up,
decapitated out of kindness
or, squeamishly sucked,
reduced to embryos.

My First Cup of Coffee

I'm sophisticated in my Cuban heels,
my mother's blue felt hat
with the smart feather like a fishing fly

as I sit with her in the Kardomah; and
coffee please, I say, not orange squash,
crossing my legs, elegant as an advert.

Beyond the ridges of my mother's perm
the High Street is a silent film
bustling with extras: hands grasping purses,

steering prams, eyes fixed on lists,
bolster hips in safe-choice-coloured skirts –
and then, centre screen, Nicolette Hawkins

(best in the class at hockey, worst at French)
and a boy – kissing,
blouse straining, hands

where they shouldn't be:
the grown-up thing. My hat's hot, silly;
coffee tastes like rust.

My mother, following my gaze, frowns: common.
I'm thinking, if I could do all that
I could be bad at French.

Erdywurble

My father's parents sold fish.
At school, Greek scholars taunted him,
the scholarship boy,
called him 'bromos', said he stank of fish.
His gifts withered; he learned
a stammer that stayed with him for life,
words jumping like the tiddlers he tried to catch
in the canal.

But from the fractured syllables, there grew
words of his own: 'Don't arrap',
he'd say when we were plaguing him.
'Pass me the erdywurble' – we in giggles
guessing what it was. 'I'm mogadored'
when the last crossword clue eluded him.
'It won't ackle', trying to splint
a broken geranium.

Unable to persuade the doctor
to help him die while he still knew himself,
his words trickled, stopped. Keening continually,
he stumbled on, mistaking night for day,
my mother for his own,
then recognising no one. Just once,
answering his new granddaughter's cry, he said
'poor kippet'.

Prognoses

'She'll walk something like this...'
Springing from his chair
he waddles, knees crumpled,
on the outer edges of his feet –
a hunchback, jester, ape,
a wind-up toy
assembled by a saboteur.
I turn away, concentrate
on the caesarean sting.

I wander corridors.

Far off, approaching,
a couple, hand in hand,
the girl, lurching
against the window's light.
I hear them laugh, pick up
the drift – a private joke,
the film they saw last night.
Long after they are gone, I hear
the jaunty click-creak of her calipers.

Intensive Care

Your voice silenced by tubes,
the mute, continual cough lifts you awake.
I stroke your hair; you stare at me,
eyes remote, tearless.

You write, 'I'm hungry.'
I watch each breath
sucked in between your ribs,
beg for you.

You lie as if in state,
too dignified.
If I thought you were leaving me
from this white room

with only plastic pillows for your journey
I would cram your hands with anemones,
snatch out the cannula, enfold you,
run with you to where the band is playing.

But now, as my hands
make shadow creatures on the wall,
I read your lips: 'rhinoceros',
know I have you still.

Getting There

Sports Day. Miss Cook
had whispered to the rest
to let you win the walking race
and not to tell.

Your jerky gait,
your straining;
the others shuffling behind,
their over-hearty cheers,

you pleased, unsure.
When your friend confessed,
wanting you to be
like anyone again,

you looked bereft,
confused
as if the walls
had changed alignment.

You understand proportion.
I still wake at night
explaining to Miss Cook
why she was wrong –

I know the artfulness
of happy endings:
once when you were small,
still chair-bound,

I dreamed you walked
perfectly into my room;
somehow, even in the dream,
a counterfeit – but so real

I woke shaking, as though
I'd almost been drawn
into a lotus-land
where I'd never find you.

Sometimes, when we're gay,
we hold hands, polka round
like dancing bears,
laughing at each other.

Broken Moon

(for Emma)

Twelve, small as six,
strength, movement, hearing
all given in half measure,
my daughter,
child of genetic carelessness,
walks uphill, always.

I watch her morning face;
precocious patience as she hooks each sock,
creeps it up her foot,
aims her jersey like a quoit.
My fingers twitch;
her private frown deters.

Her jokes can sting:
'My life is like dressed crab –
lot of effort, rather little meat.'
Yet she delights in seedlings taking root,
finding a fossil,
a surprise dessert.

Chopin will not yield to her stiff touch;
I hear her cursing.
She paces Bach exactly,
firm rounding of perfect cadences.
Somewhere inside
she is dancing a courante.

In dreams she skims the sand,
curls toes into the ooze of pools,
leaps on to stanchions.
Awake, her cousins take her hands;
they lean into the waves,
stick-child between curved sturdiness.

She turns away from stares,
laughs at the boy who asks
if she will find a midget husband.
Ten years ago,
I showed her the slice of silver in the sky.
'Moon broken,' she said.

Mother's Girl

(i.m. Pat Bain)

She remembers a mother waving from a train;
'Don't cry, silly girl,
Mother will come back very soon.'

As her life leaches out into still air
she watches tramps shuffle from the park,
knows envy's vertigo.

She hears herself speak clichés: '...a nightmare',
sees friends look reassured that dying
can be compared to anything familiar.

'The children will remember me ugly.'
But she is bone-beautiful, a Giacometti,
filigree of veins in yellowed ivory.

She wears parrot colours;
she buys great bags of tulip bulbs,
learns a new Berlioz song, talks of a holiday.

While her husband whispers to the children
she turns the fragile vaulting of her back;
marzipan smile crumbles, tastes of quinine.

A stranger's fingers clutch the furniture –
splinters, fat enough last month to draw
bravura from the piano, coax a baby into sleep.

Dressed for the ward-round she is actress
and audience, hair in a bright bandanna,
watching through ice, marionettes, miming.

Roused by a small hand from morphine dreaming
she murmurs, as she sails the summer night,
'Mother will be better, very soon.'

From Rosa in São Martinho

(for Maria Pinto)

1 *Postcard*

Looping the coast –
mountains, glint of levadas,
banana groves. So many houses!
Touch-down,
finding my face wet.

Shrieks, embraces, presents,
peeping neighbours,
maracujà, honey cake –
and noise! Night:
a lizard winking.

It has to be like this –
feeling my way
through grittiness of soap,
enamel plates, back
into the textures of home.

2 *Blessing*

Not the place I fled from –
this is a peeled, harmless replica.
I'm back, but almost as a tourist;
I don't need, after all,
the city clothes, new black suitcase
to ward off the past.

It's not that I've forgotten my father:
the burn of leather belt on skin,
fear drying the mouth like quince.
It's not that the colours – wine flush
of his eyes, neck's purple veins –
have blurred at all.

I remember how I spat him out, turned
a scarred back against him. Now, I know
I simplified him, censored the vision
of his head – pale strip of forehead
bared to the landlord, hat awkward
in his dirt-stiff hands.

But the memories are flat,
scissored frames from a lost film.
I left in silence, refused
to ask his blessing. Today, easily,
bending to kiss this tearful stranger,
I whisper 'Pai, sua benção.'

3 *Embroidery*

All day I sit cross-legged with the women
embroidering, talking of husbands –
past, present and to be arranged.
Sisters, cousin, aunts, we make the flowers
our mothers showed us, white on white.

Curved spines, rough ankles,
flattened finger-ends – their bodies
moulded to the task, they pull their threads
taut, shape disappointments
into an appliqué of laughter.

At night I hold a phantom needle,
feel my arm still lifting thread, falling.
My eye sees templates everywhere –
the sea marked out with lights of tiny boats,
the sky pricked by stars.

4 *Patching*

No real men here –
only the hopeless stay,
those softened young
by wine for wages – empty men
grown thin as clothes pegs.

Around six yesterday, my sister
laid down her needlework,
took it up, her stitches crazy,
shouted at the children,
stood waiting by the road

for Alfredo, late, staggering
arrogant as a toddler, bawling
a vicious song, wanting her

to punish. She, twice his weight,
allowed him to be strong.

Today, he stayed at home. She hid
her bruises, unpicked stitches,
fed him baby-soup. Tonight, he sits
silent, smoking harsh tobacco,
turning five escudos in his hand.

5 *Futures*

My niece walks with me in moonlight:
'I'll marry an Italian, like my aunt.
He'll be tall, blonde perhaps.
We'll ride a gondola. I'll have
a silver kitchen that works by itself.'
I squeeze her hand. I know
her mother has an eye on Paolo,
neighbour's boy – short, quiet,
working in an office in Machico.
And Fernanda's a sensible girl.

Keen for my reaction, my nephew tells me
he likes calculus. He's quick,
drums his fingers, restless for something.
I imagine him a scientist – know
he'll leave school when he can,
work for an uncle who makes coffins.
Already, in the way he turns his head,
his hooded look, angering his sisters,
there's the old pride that draws on nothing
but itself, and ends by drowning.

6 *Fish*

Shouting, they heave the dead weights
up the ramp, scales flashing,
slap them down on stones, heaped high,
spilling the smell of sea.

Women promenade, size up the catch,
begin the ancient ritual –
clamour for prices, feigned disbelief,
shrewd scrutiny of measures.

The fishermen throw down their caps,
wield hatchets, cleave great tuna
into chunks, rub salt on,
spread them in sun to dry.

My sister shows me off –
her English relative. Neighbours
dissect me with their eyes, whisper
rumours of my past.

Pride of the catch, the black espada,
ugly scabbard fish, leers
as if embarrassed at being caught
dead on a trestle table.

I stare at it: poor oddity.
In my mind's eye, its muscles
leap again; it strikes out, plunges
back to its gypsying.

7 *Photograph*

So that's who she was –
not my collage of gilded fragments,
sugar saint, eyes sea deep,
comforting me, her favourite,
but a plain girl, starved of choices,
whose bones lie hidden somewhere here
anonymous as flints.

In the creased studio photograph
there's pride, a sort of avidness
transfiguring the desperate impatience
my brother says she showed with all of us.
She poses, a star,
embracing her moment
before the shutter snapped.

I have to leave her here,
mother who never was,
be mother to myself.
But I remember reaching up
to hand her clothes-pegs,
laughing with her as we named them –
Manuel, Josè, Vicente, Father João.

8 *Orphanage*

This is where we sat
chasing lice
through one another's hair
sucking marrow bones.
Sometimes, after dark,
I'd slip out
to these plum trees,
shrunken now,
gorge stolen fruit.

I thought I'd find the faces,
frowzy veils
that stifled me for years.
But the house is empty,
stripped of the vast
camphor-smelling armoires,
credences, the cornered saints
whose monstrous shadows
subdued our urge to sing.

I hated them for their pinched
insistence on the rules.
Maybe they believed
there was no better language
they could teach a girl
than that of service,
curbing our tongues, hands, eyes –
His will be done. Today
I would have told them otherwise.

9 *Procession*

Christ, in his private ecstasy of pain,
parades the streets. The sign-writer
who retouches the gilt from time to time,
the woman who dusts Him every day
stand breathless as He passes.

Earlier they and many others knelt
as I did once, arranging lilies, agapanthus,
marigolds into a patterned carpet
which now the tubby priest,
the bearers of the statue, trample on.

We have lost touch, He and I.
I can't recapture that straightforward love,
though whether it was time, space
or experience that distanced us, who knows.
My clumsy lips shape hymns, invitations

to a place I can't climb back to.
Against the church wall, not singing,
a blind man stands alone
with outstretched hands
on which rain starts to spit.

10 *Envoi*

The engine throbs;
the island
already
foreign.

The runway
a dark finger
flicking me up,
out to sea.

Women Walking

My day is fettered by my mother's steps.
I learn the shopping list by heart,
discover architraves.
Walking this slowly
I nearly lose my balance.
I've not got that long –
at my pace I'd be going
somewhere, not marking time,
her arm locked on to mine.

*

My daughter's somewhere else.
Her tenseness fusses me
into unsteadiness.
Her arm is wooden.
Once there was suppleness,
a give and take,
a comfortable distance.
I didn't ask for this –
time, pace, speed, out of my hands.

*

Haven't we walked this way before –
a child fumbling, breathless,
clutching to keep up;
a mother tethered to a clinging hand?

Day Trip

Two women, seventies, hold hands
on the edge of Essex,
hair in strong nets,
shrieked laughter echoing gulls
as shingle sucks from under feet
easing in brine.

There must be an unspoken point
when the sea feels like
their future. No longer paddling,
ankles submerge in lace,
in satin ripple.
Dress hems darken.

They do not risk their balance
for the shimmering of ships
at the horizon's sweep
as, thigh deep, they inch on
fingers splayed, wrists bent,
learning to walk again.

Curtains

Crocheted
they censored light,
grudging flowers
stippled on the wall.

Warped hems
sealed in silence,
empty formalities
of clocks.

Steeped in vinegar,
bleached too decent
for pity or contempt,
they were veils

knotted
against curiosity,
worn enemies
of easy come and go

though cold forced entry,
its fingers
tarnishing every surface
of the room.

Perhaps they were
nourished
by the salt vapours
of her misery:

after she'd gone
their patterns
crumbled
in our hands.

Family Planning

Here is my clutch of humbugs, fickle honey-bees
swarming, sedate. Pleased to see me –
aren't you, my fondant fancies?
I want you filling every hollow of my house;
More.
Another journey to the suburbs.

I wait till after midnight,
watch bedroom lights shut off, slip
down side passages, over well-clipped lawns
searching for them. Plucking them from walls
and window sills, I tickle their ears
with tales of fish heads, drop them in my basket,
close the lid. You welcome strangers coolly
my wasps, my soft moss-agates.

I have founded a dynasty. If these pharaohs
quarrel, they turn into racoons,
tails fat with malice; I croon them
into sulky tolerance. As it grows dark
they seethe across the flagstones;
a hundred phosphorescent pools
spangle the night courtyard, pitiless.
Hunt well, my predatory loves.

At dawn the kitchen air is heavy,
moist with cat breath; on the range
the mound heaves gently,
until the hot ones struggle from beneath,
clamber on top – as, had I married,
my children might have played hand sandwiches.

Vertigo

If I should start to think too vividly
of how, while I lie here, tossing for rest,
enduring night, you, earthed at a different angle,
sit on a pine-clad hill, miles to the west

and paint the sun in wine, gaze out at peaks
adorned by ancient names; or, drunk with talk
of old times with old friends becoming old,
circle your finger with a whiskered stalk

of Rocky Mountain poppy, I should lose
my balance, slide to childhood make-believe,
step off the world's edge, plummet, fly apart
and, carried senseless in the wind's wide sleeve,

atoms of me might fall in foreign rain
defying odds, in touch with you again.

Letter from Szechuan

You cannot prevent the birds of sorrow flying over your head,
but you can prevent them building nests in your hair.
CHINESE PROVERB

Wisdom of fools and schoolmasters –
men whose heads are cabinets of drawers,
contents wax-sealed.
No purchase there for birds;
claws, sliding over perfect lacquer,
rattle the handles, bring, for a moment only,
a flutter to the dark interiors.

But we are made differently, Yi Lin.
If I could tell you of the birds,
how they have settled with me
since you were taken,
I know you would say, 'And I, and I!'
Let me write as if...

That first morning, having slept at last,
I woke to a jostle of high notes.
I felt their weight, talons
grasping loops of hair,
twisting for footholds, already tangling
strands into a nest;
crying – a narrow song,
without resolution.

I have learned their ways.
Though I cannot see them, I know
they are the colours of tarnish,
eggs heavy, leather-surfaced, rough.
They are dim-witted rather than malevolent –
pecking through my skull, not seeing
that when they have devoured hope, memory,
they will be homeless.

Birds of happiness have many songs,
these only one – my friend,
in whatever province you are lying
they sing it for you too.

Balancing Accounts

She's packed
ready to lose him
at a moment's notice.
Marching orders come
in that slight stammer
she's loved so much
in words she knows already.

She starts to speak.
He glances at the clock,
a habit she's trimmed to.
She draws together
all traces of herself.
She has a train to catch.

Or else

the sense of that bag
waiting, seeking attention,
its silent provocation
like someone
turning the first cheek,
weighs with him increasingly.

He knows her need
for ends tied up,
her inability to wear guilt
gracefully. Generous,
he sends her packing;
only, he'd be undone
by talk.

Poppies

He used arrive without no warnin'
just phone from somewhere
on the motorway. Hurry, quick
put on fresh sheets
run to Patel's – sausages, white bread
chocolate biscuits
(I think his wife a healthy livin' lady)
grab poppies from the yard
stuff them in a glass
put on dress he say he like once.

Sit and shiver. Afraid I ugly,
afraid his face fall, look aside;
no words – he don't want me
chattin' on, with him a swallow
swoopin' all over on the motorways.
Each time I forget he talk so easy.

Stories! People I never see
dance colours on the empty wall;
he make me laugh like never,
he make the stories loosen in me
only I too shy. It get late
and now poppies droopin', but he not.
He really like me, it me he lookin' at
like it the first time always.
He stroke my face, breasts, like wonder,
soft kiss my lips so they perfect.

That last time he say he love me.
He surprise as me – we both laugh.
He not come again. Ever since,
I dreamin' often I lyin' in the yard
can't move nothin', and my nipples
blossomin' with poppies.

The Uncertainty of the Poet
(after de Chirico)

1

Is there no answer to sexual obsession –
humiliation of this clown that won't lie down
but leads me to jump absurd
into unsuitable beds, leaving the Muse unserved?
O cul-de-sac delusions, love sickness
that warps imagination, subverts art.

The Corybantes knew the way of it,
those self-made eunuchs in Cybele's name –
well, my neglected and neglectful Muse,
I'll go to Dayton, Ohio. There they trap
the lecher in the brain, lobotomise…
a certain way to end the sabotage.

2

The organ withers, sleeps. My work
will flower – no women squeezing juices
that should be the Muse's. But these breasts
and broadened hips I've grown are disconcerting,
and it hurts when, hugging old friends,
I see myself reflected in their frozen eyes.

Arms, hands are a distraction. I've never doubted
that losing all libido for Her sake
will liberate great verses from my pen.
But when? My fingers ache to stroke warm flesh,
plant trees, shape earthen figures. The first step
made others easier; I'll ring Dayton, Ohio.

3

Without arms, I no longer had to play at respectable
employment. I could embrace (so to speak) the role of poet.
But bureaucrats refused to pension me
while I could walk. I could be a traffic warden,
'pleasant outdoor work'. I'd write tickets with my teeth;
they'd give a tactfully remodelled uniform.

So I've had my legs removed. It was time in any case –
for months I'd been unable to sit still. Each time
I settled at my table – torment; an unappeasable desire

97

to dance, to walk a tightrope, clamber up rocks,
dabble in foot painting...I'm one of their most
rewarding clients they tell me, here in Dayton, Ohio.

4

It's winter. They've given me a room looking out
over the plains, where I can write uninterrupted
on my remote-control word processor. Ideas spin
prosy patterns, images inane as ticker-tape,
streams of dead metaphors. Why is there no spark?
If I asked them to excise the intellect,

all senses, leaving only the heart, could I achieve
sensibility distilled, the perfect poem? Worth the price
of not being able to impart it – except to Her.
The decapitation fee here at Dayton, Ohio,
is extremely high. But I can sell my house,
my books, my – everything. I shan't be needing them.

5

They have positioned me on the terrace. I can feel sun on
my skin, though I am cold. I sense the vibration of a
distant train: the Muse, perhaps, leaving for a more fertile
climate? As my pulse slows, syncopated, I imagine next to me
phantasms of poems, clustered, like fruits: gold,
growing vigorously from the central stem. One, broken off

The Archbishop and the Cardinal

Two old men
stand in the palace garden
in their dressing-up clothes.

Hats architectural –
one a dome, the other
flying buttressed – garments

velvet, watered silk,
loops of gold chain,
these walking oxymorons

wear curious expressions –
as though the Cardinal's
found something more delicious

than the fifth deadly sin
to which his ample chasuble
bears witness.

In Lambeth back-streets
rack-rented tenants
spill on to landings.

In Liverpool
too many children
drive women mad,

while here, two old men
amble on the lawn,
landlord, father by proxy –

though it's not personal.
He might have been
a country schoolmaster

and he, with his
ruddy, potato face,
a labourer.

And these starched linens,
fine worsteds, could stand
empty, gossiping together.

Pictograph in Dust

Our land has forgotten the taste of rain,
the sky hot, scorning us for years.
We wander, settle for a time,
build houses round ourselves,
cut doors out last.

White men came on roaring carts,
showed us by signs
a different kind of place
where water leaps out of the earth
and we could live soft always.

But this is where we grew.
We are dry people, deep-rooted as thorns,
baked like our cooking-pots.
The earth holds the shape of our heels;
our ancestors need our songs.

They pointed at the sky,
played frightened, waved their arms,
then shook their heads, went away.
The land threw dust
into the air behind them.

Three dawns. Sky flash. An extra sun,
a monstrous cloud, beautiful as rain-dreams,
blossoming. We lost ourselves in looking,
lost our skin, our hair.
Was this what they were pointing to?

And lately, a new sickness.
The strangeness of it made us weep
until the elders spoke:
'All death is one,
only the tracks we take to it are different.'

Could we scratch pictures,
tell people who come after us, and after,
how the white men's spirits are terrible
to those who raise their eyes
above the thorns?

We are building our last houses –
as we have always built
but with no doors. We shall grow light,
crumble like earthenware,
become the land.

Going up the Line: Flanders

Mme Verklaede, mother of four tall sons,
hangs out washing on a fine drying day,
shirt after shirt facing the same way,
off on their anchored dance.

One, swollen with bravado,
advances towards the sky;
another writhes, reluctant to yield
to the sun's shifty blandishments.
This tattered one, a plaything for the cat,
draggles its limp sleeve along the grass.
While that one hangs crucified,
its striped brother, made of different stuff,
clowns in frantic acrobatics.
Another catches its hem on rose-thorns,
resists the summons of the wind
that makes its neighbours chatter.

Here, from beneath our feet –
were there an instrument patient enough
to tease messages along the threads –
we could exhume the uniforms,
scrape off mud, tip out the bones,
reconstitute the men who hung on them.
The biography of one nineteen-year-old
would stretch for miles
telling how he shivered that July,
played cards, wrote half-truths home,
clutched a frail talisman inside his tunic,
faint with heart-beats louder than the shells.

Mme Verklaede starts to gather up
and fold her wind-threshed harvest.
A calm evening; a faint breeze from the West
carries the bugle: the last post, from Ypres.

War Photographer

The reassurance of the frame is flexible –
you can think that just outside it
people eat, sleep, love normally
while I seek out the tragic, the absurd,
to make a subject.
Or if the picture's such as lifts the heart
the firmness of the edges can convince you
this is how things are –

as when at Ascot once
I took a pair of peach, sun-gilded girls
rolling, silk-crumpled, on the grass
in champagne giggles –

as last week, when I followed a small girl
staggering down some devastated street,
hip thrust out under a baby's weight.
She saw me seeing her; my finger pressed.

At the corner, the first bomb of the morning
shattered the stones.
Instinct prevailing, she dropped her burden
and, mouth too small for her dark scream,
began to run...

The picture showed the little mother
the almost-smile. Their caption read
'Even in hell the human spirit
triumphs over all.'
But hell, like heaven, is untidy,
its boundaries
arbitrary as a blood stain on a wall.

Graffiti

Paper having acquired a poor image,
they each in turn took a diamond stylus,
signed the treaty on a sheet of glass,
words clear against a background of red or blue.

They posed for the cameras, hair lacquered,
identical suits, each middle button fastened
to conceal the rate of respiration
and prevent any unplanned flapping of the tie.

They shook hands in ritually prescribed order,
crossing fingers in left trouser pockets
to neutralise untruth. Smiles locked in place
they saw the blood in one another's eyes.

They put on their spectacles, made speeches
(mutually incomprehensible, all equally sincere)
broadcast to the world
a sense of their historic destiny.

Then they flew home, unbuttoning their suits.
One had inscribed his name in mirror-writing.
Later, when the treaty was overturned,
he was found to be the only one on the right side.

from

CHANGING THE SUBJECT

(1990)

Driving Through France

Between croissants and croque monsieur,
in the time it takes Madame Du Plessis
to wash her coffee bowl,
take up her basket
and walk down to the shops and back,
greeting her neighbours occasionally

we have covered 174 kilometres,
passed through 23 villages
in which 237 women, 84 men and 30 dogs
were walking to the shops, or back –
and have not moved,
nor greeted anyone.

*

When I was about eight, I thought
what luck that I was born
English – not foreign
like most people in the world.

Now, flashing through yet another
undistinguished village, it strikes me
that, for some, the centre of the world
is this strip of houses called Rièstard;

whereas I know it is London
or, rather, Crouch End
or, currently,
this Ford Fiesta.

*

Here are three images:
a round bed of sunflowers in a wheat-field;
an albino boy leaning on a wall;
a pair of gates shaped like swans embracing.

Perhaps it wasn't really a flower-bed,
nor the boy really albino, nor the gates
the shape of swans. Perhaps
speed made them remarkable.

I can't return them.
I could embroider them to arbitrary life;
or file them, tokens that something happened,
like the programme from the son et lumière.

InterCity

(for Anne Harvey)

Opposite me
a fat brown man
is crying
fat glass tears
onto his Fair Isle pullover.

Needles of rain
mean–streak the landscape.
Warehouses...tower blocks...fields...
and the fat brown man
sits opposite me, crying.

Perhaps he thinks
no one will notice
if he keeps his eyes closed,
his face forced
into composure.

And everyone is
not noticing,
minding our business:
the national terror
of embarrassment

we're used to
calling tact.
Is it worse
to string the tears
into a narrative?

On Not Being a Nature Poet

Picking up a small, white feather
I note its symmetry, each tiny rib
knowing its proper measure.

I hold it in my palm, and speculate
how many I would have to balance there
before I'd feel the weight.

I see its consummate design, spare
curve like a careful hand, repelling water,
nurturing warm air.

Stroking along its spine, I like to sense
the finger-numbing softness near the root
change to resilience.

But it doesn't move me; I can't say
I love it. As I've written this, the wind
has carried it away.

Strawberries

I'm spun through time widdershins
to a room lumbered
with a childhood's furniture:
stout mahogany, teak that ousted it,
boxy armchairs, brocatelle
that smartened them as my parents
more or less kept pace with progress –
all there, sharing head-space,
colours mixed by memory to a common brown,

though outside, through French windows,
stand the well-mannered, dusty greens
of a town garden – where I hear
heels clack along the path: my mother
back from a hundred shopping trips
with some treat tucked into her basket;
and where I see my father, the day
he ran to buy me strawberries
and found it was a rag-and-bone man.

As she comes, my vague unease dissolves –
home will be home again;
and, as he does, the wrench
of wishing I could open up his hand,
show him a treat he didn't know he'd brought.

Showing

We brought our mothers' photos in
and had a show. We propped them
in a row along a shelf,
scrutinised their conformation:

Christine's, who went out to work
and voted Labour –
a straight-backed Scottish terrier,
tough and guarded.

Mrs Ascoli's borzoi profile –
taut nerves and tragedy;
exquisite in pearls and flowered straw,
head angled in the subtlest condescension.

Mary's, old and sad –
a bloodhound, hair in loops.
Jane's stocky, cheerful pug-dog of a mother
four-square with a golf-club.

Only mine was human –
a musical-box dancer
radiant in a thousand sequins.
They all agreed she was the prettiest.

Then I was ashamed I'd brought that one –
she and my father at the Ladies' Night,
eyes shining at each other;
the one that looked like history.

Birth Rite

Since I've not known another birth
this surgery seems natural.
I've left my home
and have come here
to be prepared.

You are my grail
and I must purify myself –
be stripped, shaved, emptied,
wrapped in white –
before I gain you.

Soon you'll be lifted
from the domain of wishes
and we who have been so intimate
will touch at last. Perhaps
we'll be awkward with each other.

Hiss of trolley wheels,
haze of lights...I'm drawn
through deepest passages,
protected, raised; someone
holds my hand perfectly.

To be reborn with you
I shed responsibility,
my social face,
speech, consciousness.
I reach back to the dark.

Woman Bathing in a Stream: Rembrandt

Just 'woman'.
We know it was your Hendrickje,
who bore your daughter,
reared your son,
fed you, clothed and sheltered you,
sat, stood, lay down for you,
and who, even in death,
kept you from creditors.
Almost everything we know of her
is what she did for you.

I'm angry for her –
that you took everything,
made her a vehicle for light,
shadow and reflection
and gave her only anonymity –
as now, in fashion photographs:
dress by Cardin,
hat by David Shilling,
ear-rings, necklace by Adrian Mann
and a model with no name.

Yet I can see how you refused to prettify
the ungainly shift, hoisted to hip level,
thick thighs, peasant forearms, shoulders;
how you seem to have felt their balance,
understood her spirit weight –
painted almost in her idiom.
She must have known – no wonder, then,
the serene half-smile, lack of artifice.
Being so recognised
perhaps made simple fame irrelevant.

The Balcony

(after Manet)

We form a perfect composition,
a triangle, he at the apex;
soft, glutton's hands
smelling of sandalwood and Havanas.
Though I gaze down at the street,
I know how his thumb and index finger
stroke each other, round and round,
oh, so slowly.
A woman's skin: a sheaf of banknotes.

I dig my fingers hard against my fan
to block the screaming.
I could gather up my skirts
and vault the rail;
or leap at him, plunge my nails
into those too easy going eyes.
But I sit here,
tame as this agapanthus in a pot,
central, yet marginal.

My little sister with the holy look
falters on the threshold. Will she
step on to the balcony beside me,
her cachou breath warm on my cheek?
Or will she stay, give him
that second's sweet complicity
for which he waits,
a faint flush rising,
stroking, stroking?

Girls Awake, Asleep

Young girls up all hours
devouring time-is-money on the phone:
conspiracies of mirth,
sharp analyses of friends' defects,
confession, slander, speculation –
all the little mundane bravenesses
that press the boundaries
of what can be thought, felt and talked about.
Their clear-voiced punctuation rings
up stairwells, to where parents toss
and groan, a sense of their own tolerance
some consolation for short nights, long bills.

Young girls in bed all hours
fathom sleep oceans,
drink oblivion with their deep breaths,
suck it like milk.
Curled round their own warmth,
they fat-cat on the cream of sleep
lapping dreams.
For this, they will resist all calling.
Surfing the crests of feather billows
they ride some sleek dream animal,
pulling the silk strands of his mane,
urging him on.

Piccadilly Line

Girls, dressed for dancing,
board the tube at Earl's Court,
flutter, settle.
Chattering, excited by a vision
of glitter, their fragile bodies
carry invisible antennae,
missing nothing.
Faces velvet with bright camouflage,
they're unsung stars – so young
it's thrilling just to be away from home.

One shrieks, points, springs away.
She's seen a moth
caught up in the blonde strands
of her companion's hair,
a moth, marked
with all the shadow colours of blonde.
The friend's not scared;
gently, she shakes her head,
tumbles it, dead,
into her hands.

At Piccadilly Circus they take flight,
skim the escalator,
brush past the collector,
up to the lure of light.

Christmas Circulars

This is the season when the myth-makers
play Holy Families – their filtered lives
appropriately merging with the stream
of set Nativities, Madonnas, doves.

'Robert has been promoted yet again!
We're all extremely proud of him, although
it means he has to travel quite a lot.
Sam's football-mad, but passed Grade 5 oboe.

Jean took an evening class, Renaissance art –
meals in the oven, but we were amazed
at all she knew on our super stay in Rome.
Beth triumphed in GCSE – six As!'

And from the emigrés, 'We came in June…
appalled at how run-down England's become –
no really open space…how did we stand
the weather all those years we lived in Brum?

We have a lovely place near Armidale.
Kate is the tennis champion of her school.
You wouldn't know us, we're so brown – think of us
all celebrating Christmas round the pool!'

They say, between the lines where they regret
there isn't time to write to each of us,
Our life is an accomplishment, a pearl
whose perfect shape and sheen deserve applause.

It's hard, of course. But when we see our lives
reflected here, we're almost led to think
that that's reality. So though poor Jean's
on Prozac for her nerves, and Robert drinks,

and though the children quarrel constantly
and Kate won't eat, and sometimes wets the bed,
and though we often seem to feel the draught
knife through well-fitting doors – it can't be said.

Changing the Subject

1 *The Word*

It started with my grandmother
who, fading unspeakably,
lay in the blue room; disappeared
leaving a cardboard box,
coils of chalky-brown rubber tube.

I inherited her room, her key.
The walls were papered bright
but the unsayable word
seeped through; some nights
I heard it in the dripping of the tap.

I saw it in my parents' mouths,
how it twisted lips for whispers
before they changed the subject.
I saw it through fingers
screening me from news.

The word has rooted in my head
casting blue shadows.
It has put on flesh,
spawned strong and crazy children
who wake, reach out their claws.

2 *Out-Patients*

Women stripped to the waist,
wrapped in blue,
we are a uniform edition
waiting to be read.

These plain covers suit us:
we're inexplicit,
it's not our style to advertise
our fearful narratives.

My turn. He reads my breasts
like braille, finding the lump
I knew was there. This is
the episode I could see coming –

although he's reassuring,
doesn't think it's sinister
but just to be quite clear...
He's taking over,

he'll be the writer now,
the plot–master,
and I must wait
to read my next instalment.

3 *Diagnosis*

He was good at telling,
gentle, but direct;
he stayed with me
while I recovered breath,
started to collect

stumbling questions. He said
cancer with a small c –
the raw stuff of routine –
yet his manner showed
he knew it couldn't be ordinary for me.

Walking down the road
I shivered like a gong
that's just been struck –
mutilation...what have I done...
my child...how long... –

and noticed how
the vast possible array
of individual speech
is whittled by bad news
to what all frightened people say.

That night, the freak storm.
I listened to trees fall,
stout fences crack,
felt the house shudder as the wind
howled the truest cliché of them all.

4 *In-Patient*

I have inherited another woman's flowers.
She's left no after-scent, fallen hairs,
no echoes of her voice,
no sign of who or how she was

or through which door she made her exit.
Only these bouquets – carnations,
tiger lilies, hothouse roses,
meretricious everlasting flowers.

By day, they form the set in which I play
the patient – one of a long line
of actresses who've played the part
on this small white stage.

It's a script rich in alternatives.
Each reading reveals something new,
so I perform variously – not falsehoods,
just the interpretations I can manage.

At night, the flowers are oracles.
Sometimes they seem to promise a long run;
then frighten me with their bowing heads,
their hint of swan-songs.

5 *Woman in Pink*

The big, beautiful copper-haired
woman in the next bed
is drowning in pink.

She wears pink frills,
pink fluffy cardigan and slippers.
Her 'get well' cards carry pink messages.

Her husband brings pink tissues,
a pink china kitten; he pats her head.
She speaks in a pink powder voice.

Yet she is big and beautiful and coppery.
At night, she cries bitterly,
coughs and coughs from her broad chest.

They've done all they can.
She's taking home bottles of morphine syrup,
its colour indeterminate.

6 *How Are You?*

When he asked me that
what if I'd said,
rather than 'very well',
'dreadful – full of dread'?

Since I have known this,
language has cracked,
meanings have re-arranged;
dream, risk and fact

changed places. Tenses tip,
word–roots are suddenly
important, some grip
on the slippery.

We're on thin linguistic ice
lifelong, but I see through;
I read the sentence
we are all subject to

in the stopped mouths of those
who once were 'I',
full-fleshed, confident
using the verb 'to die'

of plants and pets and parents
until the immense
contingency of things
deleted sense.

They are his future
as well as mine,
but I won't make him look.
I say, 'I'm fine'.

7 *Anna*

Visiting time. Anna rises from her bed,
walks down the ward, slowly,
treading glass. She wears
her hand-sewn patchwork dressing-gown,
cut full, concealing her swollen abdomen.

She smiles at people she passes;
pulls her shoulders back,
making a joke about deportment;
waves a skeletal hand
at Mrs Shah, who speaks no English.

Her little girls sit by her bed
in their school uniforms. Too good,
they're silent as they watch her,
tall in her brave vestment
of patterned tesserae

that once were other garments –
as she was: a patchwork mother
made of innumerable creative acts
which they'll inherit with her robe
and make of them something new.

She stops. We hold our breath.
Gaining time, she whispers to a nurse
then turns, walks back to her children,
smiling. Look, she is telling them,
I'm still familiar. I belong to you.

8 *Knowing Our Place*

Class is irrelevant in here.
We're part of a new scale –
mobility is all one way
and the least respected
are envied most.

First, the benigns,
in for a night or two,
nervous, but unappalled;
foolishly glad their bodies
don't behave like that.

Then the exploratories;
can't wait to know, but have to.
Greedy for signs, they swing
from misery to confidence,
or just endure.

The primaries are in
for surgery – what kind? What then?
Shocked, tearful perhaps;
things happening too fast.
Still can't believe it, really.

The reconstructions are survivors,
experienced, detached.
They're bent on being almost normal;
don't want to think
of other possibilities.

Secondaries (treatment)
are often angry – with doctors, fate –
or blame themselves.
They want to tell their stories,
not to feel so alone.

Secondaries (palliative)
are admitted swathed in pain.
They become gentle, grateful,
they've learned to live
one day at a time.

Terminals are royalty,
beyond the rest of us.
They lie in side-rooms
flanked by exhausted relatives,
sans everything.

We learn the social map
fast. Beneath the ordinary chat,
jokes, kindnesses, we're scavengers,
gnawing at each other's histories
for scraps of hope.

9 *Difficult Passages*

'You did not proper practise,'
my cello teacher's sorrowful
mid-European vowels reproached me.
'Many times play through the piece
is not the proper practising –
you must repeat difficult passages
so when you make performance
there is no fear – you know
the music is inside your capacity.'
Her stabbing finger, moist gaze,
sought to plant the lesson in my soul.

I've practised pain for forty years –
all those Chinese burns;
the home-made dynamo we used
to test our tolerance for shocks;
hands wrapped round snowballs;
untreated corns – all pain practice.
Fine – if I can choose the repertoire.
But what if some day I'm required
to play a great pain concerto?
Will that be inside my capacity?

10 *Outside*

I've hung the washing out
and turn to see
the door slammed shut
by a capricious wind.

Locked out, face to the glass,
I see myself reflected
in the mirror opposite,
framed, slightly menacing.

No need for wuthering
to feel how it might be –
I have that sepia, far-seeing
look of long-dead people.

Perhaps I wouldn't feel dead,
just confused, lost track of time;
could it be years since I turned
with that mouthful of pegs?

And might I now beat on the glass
with jelly fists, my breath
making no cloud in this crisp air,
shout with no sound coming?

Death could seem this accidental –
the play of cells
mad as the freakishness of weather,
the arbitrary shutting out.

Might there be some self left
to look back, register
the shape of the receding house?
And would it feel this cold?

11 *Choosing the Furniture*

The curtains said:
what do you fear more than anything?
Look at it now.

A white room.
I lie and cannot speak,
can not get up.
I stream with pain from every part.
I cry, scream until the sound chokes me.
Someone at the door looks in,
glances at her watch, moves on.
No one comes. No one
will ever come.

The lamp said:
think of what would be most blissful –
what do you see?

A white room
lined with books; a window
looking out on trees and water;
bright rugs, a couch, a huge table
where I sit, words spinning from my fingers.
No one comes; time is limitless,
alone is perfect.
Someone leaves food at the gate –
fruit, bread, little chocolate birds.

The moon laughed:
there is only one room.
You choose the furniture.

12 *I Shall Paint My Nails Red*

because a bit of colour is a public service.

because I am proud of my hands.

because it will remind me I'm a woman.

because I will look like a survivor.

because I can admire them in traffic jams.

because my daughter will say ugh.

because my lover will be surprised.

because it is quicker than dyeing my hair.

because it is a ten-minute moratorium.

because it is reversible.

13 *Watching Swallows*

In my fiftieth year,
with my folded chin
that makes my daughter call me Touché Turtle;

in my fiftieth year,
with a brood of half-tamed fears
clinging around my hem,

I sit with my green shiny notebook
and my battered red notebook
and my notebook with the marbled cover,

and I want to feel
revolutions spinning me apart,
re-forming me –

as would be fitting in one's fiftieth year.

Instead, I hum a tune to my own pulse.

Instead, I busy dead flies off the sill
and realign my dictionaries.

Instead, through the window,
I make a sign of solidarity
at swallows, massing along the wires.

Visiting Duncan

(for Nancy Stepan)

I'm on a day trip to our shared frontier,
pass tissue-wrapped daffodils, chocolate
across the gap; my greeting warm, but careful,
taking the measure of your foreignness.
How far have you travelled

in your migration to that other country
whose landscape, customs, I can only guess?
It's an America, dividing you from me
by language much like mine, yet skewed,
stripped. I make conversation:

'Nurse says you went to Hastings yesterday –
I wonder if you remember...'
'Was it meant to be memorable?' you ask,
not meaning, I think, to be witty
though later I'll laugh, remembering.

You don't talk about the old country,
little of the new – as you did once
when contrast, loss, were everything.
The discourse you've learned here
is that of emptiness.

You examine the dimensions of the void
with all your old precision; picking up
a letter from your son, 'Do I miss him?
What would be the test? Do I wish
he were here? I think not.'

A woman comes into your room. 'I have
nothing', she says. Just that, twice,
and leaves. Later, another: 'I'm so hungry –
can you give me food...nothing all day.'
You break her off some chocolate.

'It's an existence'. You leave
the alternative unsaid. Your final exile
has no reference points; in an hour
you won't know I was here. There's only now;
this only kiss; these hands, holding.

The Bed

When they were young, and she a captive
in her parents' house, he'd climb
in through her window. They'd whisper,
touch, slip together in her narrow bed
until the rooster pulled them separate
and sent him, singing, to the field.

Their marriage bed was ample.
Child after child was born in it
until, pushed to the side, he played
the hero in the field, the tavern.
Resentments multiplied; the bed was
for sleeping, back towards back, alone.

In middle age, as she gained flesh,
he lightened, rolled towards the centre.
One night, he floated from his dream,
found her arm curved around him,
hand tucked under his side,
and she was murmuring an old song.

In their seventies, he took a saw,
halved the bed's width. Climbing in
earlier each day, they found
a dozen different ways of fitting,
fusing at last into a shape so right
they felt no further need to move apart.

Ruby Wedding

Forty years this month
since you hurtled round the corner
into me, taking my breath away.

Eye-watering you were
like lemons after long thirst,
a burst of bubbles.

I'd learned to patch my emptiness
with tidy habits,
was comforted by order,

but you – a bouquet of astonishments
a chaos I fought
then learned to mingle with.

Sometimes I'd watch you sleeping,
switchback your breath – even then
you seemed so vivid.

I'd rub your hands
skin turning to plastic, paper,
then to ash.

As I've cleared
your squirrelled papers, ornaments,
order has ticked back into every room.

I have been slow
to cast off from the bed
in which we joined and parted

but now I'm drifting out.
You have breathed my last breath.
My heart is jumping for the two of us.

Partners

It was always said – she
was the strong one,
the emphasis implying
something not quite natural.

It showed in her head's angle
inherited from a line of officers
khaki-convincing in the gallery
of family photographs.

She always knew her mind.
He never could decide on anything.
After he died, people said
she'd grown to look like him –

as if his soul, lacking direction,
had managed a short hop
and settled in that softening jaw,
that bewilderment behind the eyes.

Reflections

Looking for myself
I creep from one reflection to the next.
I stare; I see
suggestions of my son, my granddaughter.
I'm not there –

though if I should bend this way, and this,
couldn't I curve back to the place
where the first mirror surely held me
in perfect, loving, infinite regard?

I'm drawn to any shiny surface –
the polished floor, a silver horn,
windows in a revolving door.
They're never right, never
that milk-blue light I'm longing for.

Often I'm only smudges
or scattered by cracks;
but I'm there at least,
I've some hold on the ground I trod
before I found out what I lacked,
and what the mirror did.
And what the mirror
did.

Für Therese

I'll tell you why –

You must understand, since he died
he has that special unreality
that greatness gives; as if he's been distilled
into his Ode to Joy, his Grosse Fuge.

I knew a different man – an embarrassment
to good society, gauche beyond belief!
Tone-poet he may have been, but blind
to the shadow of reproof in Father's eye –
he would hold forth about that Bonaparte.
Almost a child – he'd know he'd caused offence
but not know how, nor how to put it right.

And yet, he altered when we were alone.
He loved me, and I felt for once
powerful – great temptation to a girl
expected to transform from father's daughter
into husband's wife. But then I saw
how we'd grow disappointed with each other –
he with my limited capacity
to understand his art; I with his constant
absence in a world that shut me out.

Frau van Beethoven! Now I'm facing death
I sometimes whisper to myself that title,
missed, and wonder if I could have learned

enough to follow him…but after all
our names were not intended to be linked –
even the little piece he wrote for me
that might have been my mark on history,
his publisher misread as *Für Elise*.

Why I Lie in This Place

We were close once.
I knew him better than I knew myself –
the way his lips tensed when he was moved,
his knack with children,
the smell of his sweat mingled with the horses'
after a fast ride together.

I made no secret of it.
I heard the envious sniggering,
but I sought him out, and he, me,
I swear it. We drank and whored together.
We discussed court business,
talked sport and strategy –

until he changed. In such little ways
at first, mere moments of distraction,
the smile a shade less warm – I didn't think.
And then, as I was talking once, I caught
a glance, thrown by him to his equerry,
as if to say 'that's typical, you see'

and the world somersaulted – suddenly
no longer partner, fellow-witness,
but object, irreversibly split off.
I left the city then, grew hard.
Indifferent to death, I flourished
in far-flung campaigns.

The people sought me out, asked me
to lead the revolt against him. I'd heard
he had become cruel, a voluptuary –
they had real grievances. And yet
their quarrel wasn't mine. Had it not been
for that flick of the eyelid –

the hinge on which hung
love and hate, peace and war, the fate
of princedoms and ten thousand little lives –
I'd have bent my strength to his;
what followed would have happened differently.
As it was, I used the masses' anger –

or was it the reverse?
Perhaps the swell of history
would have rolled on without my part in it.
I only know, but for that look,
these many hundred years,
I should have been lying next to him.

The Chairman's Birthday

The day before, my father
had visited the butcher's shop himself
to choose the calf's head.

Our pastry cook was gone
(I hadn't thought of him as an Enemy)
so the dessert course would be ordinary.
But the calf's head! Father's speciality.

He held it up to admire its whiteness;
I shunned its eyes, its open baby mouth.
He plunged it in the bubbling pan
covered closely with a piece of cloth
to stop it turning black.

Meanwhile the sauce – Madeira demi-glace –
quenelles of minced truffles,
sautéed cocks' combs...

and when the head was lifted steaming,
placed on a platter, he surrounded it
with mushrooms, halves of hard-boiled egg,
sweetbreads, its own sliced tongue and brains,
poured on the sauce, carried it, glistening,
ceremoniously to table.

*

Because they took him two days later
that evening runs on a continuous reel
inside my head; a melodrama lit by Eisenstein.

Under the chandeliers
Father walks, bearing the dish,
to comic tuba music – though then
it seemed triumphal, dignified.

Cut to the Chairman, who shifts his eyes
as he thanks Father for the feast
while quavering violins,
my father's sweating, deferential forehead,
seem to interrogate the future
and find their own reply.

And then the epilogue –
because I've wondered ever since
if he had slaughtered me,
served me with miraculous garnishes,
could he be living now?

Ghost Stations

We are the inheritors. We hide here
at the roots of the perverted city
waiting, practising the Pure Way.
Listening to ourselves, each other,
we find the old soiled words won't do;
often we can only dance our meanings.

Deep in the arteries of London, life
is possible – in the forgotten stations:
York Road, St Mary's, Seething Lane...
I love the names. Each day, we sing them
like a psalm, a celebration –
Down Street, British Museum, City Road.

We live on waste. After the current's off
we run along tunnels, through sleeping trains,
ahead of the night cleaners. We find chips,
apple cores (the most nutritious part),
dregs of Coke. On good days, we pick up
coins that fit the chocolate machines.

Once I found a whole bag of shopping.
That night we had an iceberg lettuce,
a honeydew melon, tasting of laughter.
And once, an abutilon – its orange
bee-flowers gladdened us for weeks.
Such things are dangerous;

now, to remind ourselves, we read
the newspapers we use as mattresses,
or gather on the platforms,
witness the trains as they rip past
(our eyes have grown used to the speed).
Almost every known depravity

is acted out on trains – rape, drunkenness,
robbery, fighting, harassment, abuse.
And the subtler forms – intellectual bullying,
contempt, all the varieties of indifference...
We've learned to read the faces;
we need to see these things, simply.

The travellers only see their own reflections.
But lately, a few in such despair
they cup their faces to the glass, weeping,
have seen the ghost stations
and though we're always out of sight,
they sense our difference and find their way.

Our numbers are growing, though there are
reverses. Some lose heart, want to leave.
We can't let them – we keep them all
at Brompton Road, carefully guarded,
plotting uselessly, swapping fantasies,
raving of sunlight, mountains or the sea.

One day, we'll climb out, convert the city!
The trains are full of terrible energy;
we only have example, words. But there is
our chant to strengthen us, our hope-names:
Uxbridge Road, King William Street,
South Kentish Town, South Acton, Bull and Bush…

Night Harvest
(for Martin)

We dredge these small fry
from our separate pools of sleep,
spread them before each other

and sort them, puzzling,
smiling to discover
our several selves in them.

Under water their colours
were subtly different.
Some slipped back as we lifted them

but these are enough, prismatic,
splitting the past, the future
into bright fragments.

We can afford to be extravagant,
throw back the catch,
know it will multiply.

from

STRIKING DISTANCE

(1994)

This Morning

Creation might have been like this,
early sun stencilling the leaves
of the first ever walnut trees,
and the cows beside them splashes
of caramel, coffee, apricot, vanilla,
drifting as if under water
in breeze-fractured light.

I have the eyes of the academy,
mince the natural world into word-burgers
seasoned with disappointment.
These lovely prelapsarian cows
are a poem, generous in conception,
perfectly achieved, rhythms,
rhyming, untranslatable.

My gaze makes them alien to themselves.
Bashful, they shift their stout elegance,
breathe soft, uneasy huffs, wrestling
with doubt. But as the church clock strikes
seven, twice over, we are between times,
and simply the world's new inhabitants
staring at the other, staring.

Waiting Room

It was slippery blind surfaces,
rushing waterways, a distant drum.

It was drifting at anchor, warm
power of stretch and kick.

Sometimes, there was red to dance to,
and songs: mother-sounds without edges.

I'd answer, but nothing came.
My lips were always practising.

A mouth-fit thumb or a toe
would come to console me.

A time of loud words bruising
against each other; then a giddy shock

hurled me against the dim-lit screen,
unharmed, but understanding I didn't have

the temperament for silent suffering,
that this was the moment to

take on gravity, to haul myself
round, and out on a tide of cries.

The Fall

The rest of your life starts
when a world of snug non-sense
you've not imagined could be otherwise
turns mean, and there you are,
the usual you and getting
smacked for it, not understanding why.

Did you dream rusks, pat-a-cake, the bliss
you summoned when you squeezed your eyes?
Now smiles are weather.
You learn rain-dance and ritual,
slant looks, pent farts,
the cussedness of spoon and fork.

So much forbidden, you never know all
the names for it. You punish your dolls
for their mistakes, and feel quite cheerful;
only sometimes there's a pellet in your mouth
you can't spit out or swallow,
the bitterness of crusts you're stuck with.

Passed On

Before, this box contained my mother.
For months she'd sent me out for index cards,
scribbled with a squirrel concentration
while I'd nag at her, seeing strength
drain, ink-blue, from her finger-ends
providing for a string of hard winters
I was trying not to understand.

Only after, opening it, I saw
how she'd rendered herself down from flesh
to paper, alphabetical; there for me
in every way she could anticipate
— *Acupuncture: conditions suited to*
— *Books to read by age twenty-one*
— *Choux pastry: how to make, when to use.*

The cards looked after me. I'd shuffle them
to almost hear her speak. Then, my days
were box-shaped (or was I playing safe?)
for every doubt or choice, a card that fitted
— *Exams: the best revision strategy*
— *Flowers: cut, how to make them last*
— *Greece: the men, what you need to know.*

But then they seemed to shrink. I'd turn them over,
find them blank; the edges furred, mute,
whole areas wrong, or missing. Had she known?
The language pointed to what wasn't said.
I'd add notes of my own, strange beside
her urgent dogmatism, loosening grip
— *infinitives never telling love*
  lust single issue politics when
  don't hopeless careful trust.

On the beach, I built a hollow cairn,
tipped in the cards. Then I let her go.
The smoke rose thin and clear, slowly blurred.
I've kept the box for diaries, like this.

146

Coat for an Undergraduate

From Italy, by way of Harrods.
I snatched it from a wealthy tourist,
this perfect coat, size 9-10 years,
wool and cashmere, silk, exquisite detail.
It flared as I revolved it on its hanger,
deep folds embracing light.

We're excited by it – the cut, the cost.
Aren't we both imagining
it will make you, too, perfect,
propel you down the Broad firm-footed,
give you stature,
free all stiffnesses?

On you, the hem dips,
shoulders poke, empty,
top button, unmanageable.
I rage as I pick open seams,
pin, tack, cut, cack-handed,
compromise the marvellous finish.
Your whole life make do,
never mended enough.

Look – in the country of the possible,
this is a real transformation.
Child-sized you may be, but here is
your come-of-age reflection;
and you're thinking tall
as you drive away in your red car,
green boots, and the perfect enough coat,
swinging, sock-it-to-them, classy blue.

File Past

While his back's turned I slip inside
my pink, fat file,
the cover flopping shut behind me.
It's hot, airless.

I start to chew through layers of forms,
letters, case conference reports,
leaving a hole the size of me.
I get thirsty.

I notice names. Muscles twitch,
remembering – eyelids, anus, fists.
Such a little hand. Put it here.
Love. Aah. Mustn't tell or. Love

I bite through love
and all the other vomit words –
Security, Care, Sharing, Come to terms –
I can only say with a funny accent.

My name is scattered everywhere
but I'm not in this wad of bits,
this People In My World diagram,
Life Story Book (my life, their story).

Here is a girl who glares with my eyes;
weird clothes, greasy hair, my sort of age –
my mother there are almost no names left for.
Ref. file CP 62/103.

You Make Your Bed

You make your bed, precisely not to lie on it
but to confine the disorder of the night
in mitred corners, unruffled surfaces.

Morning's already clamouring in your head.
This is a stand against incompetence,
at least one perfectly accomplished act.

All day it's what you've put behind you,
an infant place that, with the dark, draws you
down, and back; an enticing book

whose soft covers you open, slipping into
those quotidian rehearsals – love
and sleep. And dream irresponsibly

until the bell clangs for the next round.
Loath to climb out, you know you should be glad
you can. You make your bed precisely.

Skin Distance

Can you imagine this?

You're sitting on the tube
opposite a strapping lad, black,
late teens, seventeen stone-ish.
You haven't noticed him particularly
until he fetches out a jar of
baby-food (creamed carrots),
levers the lid off with his teeth,
spoons up large mouthfuls.

Urgently now, he follows
with turkey dinner, banana delight
sunshine breakfast, rice and pears...

And you're feeling queasy, seeing
who you are is accidental
and there's only a couple of skins
between being you, and tipping over

into the life of a young, black, male,
seventeen-stone baby-food junkie
who doesn't seem to care who notices
or what they're thinking.

Can you feel the slither of semolina
creeping across your tongue,
your limbs becoming heavier?

Tide, Turning

Sliced flat, androgynous,
a child again with all to play for,
I've come here to encounter the sea.

Clownish, she catches me out, slap on the back
no joke – though I laugh
spluttering while she collapses in ripples.

Mother, she rocks me on her slack, dark breast.
She's quickly bored,
spits in my eye, fiddles with my hair.

Lover with a wicked past, her licks
and soft caresses turn to rough trade
throwing me off balance.

I am a fish she'll try to suck
down to her pebble bed; I am a rod
erect as she curls above me.

Too quick for her – I slice across
her oily invitation, and up
through shards of savage light.

She cuffs me to size
with her grey, glass paw
reminding me who was here first –

and will be here, long after
anyone who reckons she's paid off
her debt to the moon.

Gifts

When I think of her, I see that swift
flick of her hair,
how she'd stroke it, brush it
lowering her head to where the light
sought out the shine.
She called it her gift.

There was a way she lived in music, rare,
like her last illness.
Her keyboard brilliance
was unremarkable to her – as I
might think of speaking;
or of hair.

Perhaps because by then she had begun
to see it fall
to medical heroics,
she loved it more than gifts she'd only lose
when étude, fugue and hair
would be all one.

Or maybe, in the mirror, her eyes met
the aureole,
brighter than she could bear,
of an enormity – so that she fastened
onto her hair's lustre
all value, all regret.

Woman in Brown

Woman in brown
almost not there at all;
a shadow, shadowless
propped into a chair against the wall;
eyes, semi-breves,
wrists hanging slack:
anaglyptic undersides of leaves.

Imagine her against light – there,
where sun is shafting through the door.
You'd see through skin
to peristalsis, respiration,
the automatic busyness of circulation –
a clock in a deserted house;
action there's no longer reason for.

But for a chance ordering of matter
this woman might have been
me. But she is the one in brown
and I can wrap her up in words,
drive back to town
as her thoughts leak gently out
to blizzard on the television screen.

Presents for Duncan

Ten years ago, I could have brought a book
of Gramsci's, say, or Larkin's. You'd have asked
my views on Europe, taken me to look
at a new camellia; maybe we'd have driven
somewhere for a concert – Bach or Bruch.

Even last year, there might have been a walk,
you in a wheelchair, through the ordered grounds
to the pub beyond the gate. Then, you could talk
about the people in old photographs,
and tell a kestrel from a sparrowhawk.

Opportune, that in middle age we're blind
to future selves, will not imagine some
arterial sabotage could make a mind
that rocketed shrink to random sparks
(since entropy's impartially unkind).

Today, as you catch sight of me, you scream
and wail, knowing yourself, in that moment,
lost. Then reaching, parrot-slow, you seem
content to cram your mouth with an old sweetness:
all the world in a chocolate orange cream.

Death Speaks after the Tone

What shall I say to you,
your uni-person voice designed to suit
sales-people, colleagues, closest friends, your son?
You must see it won't do

for me, who know you best.
I was there before you knew yourself.
I understand the fluxion of your heart,
its innermost recess.

'I'm not here right now' –
technology leads you to murder sense.
Or is it fear makes you indifferent
to what words say, and how?

If you'd allow me in,
let me speak directly to you, soon
you'd see I am essential to your life,
its spiritual twin.

You think you'll put me off
if you cower behind that amputated voice
there, not there, never there for me.
But I've time enough.

I'll never go away.
I'll be here, pressed against your grille,
smoked glass, net curtain of a voice,
day after day after day.

The Way We Live Now

I'm walking into *La Porchetta*
with Daughter and ex-Husband
when I spot ex-Lover and new woman
sharing a tricolore salad, mozzarella
soaring mouthwards on a single fork.

I think I'm going to faint, but instead
stroll across, force an introduction.
She has strong hair, a usurper's handshake
and 'nice to meet you', she says,
dabbing at her cerise pearl lips

I retreat with grace to where D
and ex-H can report on how ex-L
and companion are arranging their faces.
I play with my spaghetti marinara;
concentrate on other fish.

The man at the next table tells us he's
my ex-husband's ex-lover's ex-husband:
Neil. Over an espresso, he announces
he's rethought his fellow-travelling
with feminism. He seems to want applause.

My ex knows Neil's ex- and current wives
are planning to move in together.
I know my ex-lover's woman is getting
in touch with her Inner Child and is giving
ex-L a hard time. Though not hard enough.

My daughter knows everything.

Where Are You

In this garden, after a day of rain,
a blackbird is taking soundings,
flinging his counter-tenor line
into blue air, to where
an answering cadenza shows
the shape and depth of his own solitude.

Born in South London, inheritors
of brick, smoke, slate, tarmac,
uneasy with pastoral
as hillbillies with high-rise,
my parents called each other
in blackbird language:
my father's interrogative whistle
– 'where are you?'
my mother's note, swooping, dutiful
– 'here I am'.

There must have slid into the silences
the other questions,
blind, voiceless worms whose weight
cluttered his tongue;
questions I hear as, half a lifetime on,
I eavesdrop on blackbirds.

Moment

Driving to meet you,
a scent surfacing
in the mind –
a random pulse
leaping the wrong synapse –

the trace
of another life –
gunpowder, was it,
or hot vanilla –

overturned the furniture
of love,
as a shaft of air
from an opened window
enlarges an over-heated room.

Our Peacock

He was a gloss on that English garden of roses,
banks of blowsy peonies, clipped box.
Ours, because we were his only audience,
and one of us, at least, wanting him to be
an oracle, to fill the sad silence between us
with a fanful of gorgeous air, a sign
richer than the sun's feeble water-dance.

Chivvied by a dozen bloomered bantams,
he dragged his train sulkily in the dust,
a legendary actor in a fit of temperament;
but turned then and, with a shiver of quills,
displayed his gifts to us, no holding back;
Platonic peacock strutting his stuff, all symmetry,
brilliancies, rank upon rank of exquisite eyes.

It wasn't nothing, that we were sharing this
in an English garden smelling of lavender.
But his cold glance told me there's no beauty,
anywhere, to set against old failures of love.
As we left, he lifted himself high into a tree,
and cried out; his voice, broken glass
tearing the heart out of the afternoon.

One

Those are the worst times.
Not the cold
ghost at my back
when I turn in the small hours;

not the fury with myself
and you when the screwdriver's
wrong and my hand stumbles
and bleeds;

but after I've halved
the last piece of walnut cake,
or marked in the paper
something that would amuse you

or, at the sales, dithered
over whether you'd like
the check or the blue best –
the small ways

I assume you – then
the Oh, like an uppercut.
And look
I'm talking to you.

Out of Reach

Raja...puja...
a Tamil song,
catchy in a Madras taxi,
seemed, in the space between near-misses,
to connect the driver's torn shirt,
the bullet-proof vest of the State governor,
quilts fitting the humped backs of cattle.

It's gone
leaving only its impression.
Asking in the music shop
I offer Raja...puja...
as a baby mouths urgent syllables
at kindly adults
deaf to the most important thing.

Crossing the Border

This cake I'm making –
I'd rather do almost anything else
but I need a place for these ingredients.

Elsewhere, another woman risks
a shell-gashed balcony to light a fire.
She guides a baby's thumb into its mouth.

My cake is made of dry and wet elements.
The god of the fleeting moment
blesses them into something new.

She has boiled pasta, a handful
for her family of four; a smear
of mustard. They call it soup.

This cake is made of such plenty
yet it won't rise.
I mean it as an offering

but how can it fit into a time
of bread in the wrong places,
of no – no more – nothing?

If I could, I'd walk with it
across the map of Europe,
over bland pastels, wavering boundaries,

to where she's silent as a man says,
I won't die of death, but of
Love For My City.

*

Children come like sparrows to my table
flight upon flight; cold
fingers grasp the hard edge,
nails scrabbling for grains of salt.

I eat my warm, rich food. Every day
they have a more migrant look.
Above them, the funeral bird
strops a complacent beak.

Sanity would turn time
back on itself, reel the children in,
to stack them
in vast ovarian warehouses, sleeping.

Let their next life be as meadow larks –
their high, clean thatness;
dying just deaths
unfreighted by love, pride, consequence.

Striking Distance

Was there one moment when the woman
who's always lived next door turned stranger
to you? In a time of fearful weather
did the way she laughed, or shook out her mats
make you suddenly feel as though
she'd been nursing a dark side to her difference
and bring that word, in a bitter rush
to the back of the throat – *Croat/ Muslim/
Serb* – the name, barbed, ripping
its neat solution through common ground?

Or has she acquired an alien patina
day by uneasy day, unnoticed
as fallout from a remote explosion?
So you don't know quite when you came to think
the way she sits, or ties her scarf,
is just like a Muslim/Serb/Croat;
and she uses their word for water-melon
as usual, but now it's an irritant
you mimic to ugliness in your head,
surprising yourself in a savage pleasure.

Do you sometimes think, she could be you,
the woman who's trying to be invisible?
Do you have to betray those old complicities –
money worries, sick children, men?
Would an open door be too much pain
if the larger bravery is beyond you
(you can't afford the kind of recklessness
that would take, any more than she could);
while your husband is saying you don't understand
those people/Serbs/Muslims/Croats?

One morning, will you ignore her greeting
and think you see a strange twist to her smile –
for how could she not, then, be strange to herself
(this woman who lives nine inches away)
in the inner place where she'd felt she belonged,
which, now, she'll return to obsessively
as a tongue tries to limit a secret sore?
And as they drive her away, will her face
be unfamiliar, her voice, bearable:
a woman crying, from a long way off?

Advent in Bratislava 1992
(for Michael Rustin)

Ten days to New Year, the fog's cold comfort
paints the square non-commital.
This passes for a market, ramshackle piles
of moist acrylic sweaters, glass baubles.
Children, like children anywhere,
suck chemical lollipops, staring
at the fog-wrapped, festive tree.

To us, from a more electric city,
this is a place in hibernation,
smatterings of light snuffed easily,
shops, cafés, turned inwards, as if refusing
to whore for passing trade, to get the hang
of the bland competence that's ordinary
up river, and points west.

We're plump with bright ideas, but this
is not the season for practicalities.
In the wedding cake Filharmonia,
fin de siècle bourgeois look-alikes,
treading the frayed red carpet, stroll
through the interval; their apparatchik past
tucked under their tongues, dissolving slowly.

Thanatos

Small again, I was pitting my mute will
against the clash of parents who held
the universe between them.

This time, though, the whole sky
was a battlefield for kamikaze planets
careening in a wide lens – bodies

sucking substance from each other
like punished souls caught, for want of pity,
in a timeless passion for each other's harm.

Earth was part of it, with Mars,
its swelling shadow our prognosis.
Half awake, I felt the world's oceans

pitch and slop in the huge bowl
of my arms. Around me lay oblivious cities
and I was straining to hold steady, steady.

There Will Come a Time
(from Marina Tsvetaeva)

There will come a time, lovely creature,
when I shall be for you – a distant trace
lost in the blue pools of your memory.
You will forget my aquiline profile,
forehead wrapped in a halo of cigarette smoke,
the perpetual laugh I use to hoodwink people,
the hundred silver rings on my tireless hand,
this attic crow's-nest, the sublime confusion
of my papers.   You will not remember
how, in a terrible year, raised up by Troubles,
you were little.   And I was young.

[November 1919]

167

America

(for Eva Hoffman)

That was a haloed sound
the soft, crisp grace of it
held on the lips,
unfolding into space –
America!

We embarked in new clothes,
the plainest. We'd burned
the old, along with our sins,
all complicated, sad relations,
all slant, avaricious things.

Spring, and a following wind.
We almost rejoiced in spewing up
our very linings, as the gale
big-bellied the mainsail,
caked our hair white.

Our thoughts flew forwards,
singing. Had I understood
there is no innocence
like that of a long journey,
I might have dreaded landfall.

America – raccoon, cardinals,
new colours in the earth.
We trekked through summer,
guided to the place
we called Redemption.

All our wants were wants
for all of us. We were re-made
by daily quartering of bread;
scars, callouses in common.
We were perfected. Prospered...

Hard to say in whose bones
the seed of Self had lain like
tubercle. Slowly, we've sickened,
and with diseases one can't name
except by absence.

Our lips are flaking
as we creep into familiar rags
we don't acknowledge. We've become
all closed hands, faces, doors.
I can't live with no America.

The Trial of Lyman Atkins

Where he lives, they get along without them,
words. Him and his brothers. Just soft names
to coax the heifers out frosty mornings;
gabble, gabble, laughter teasing the turkeys;
once a month, greeting folks in the farmstore.

So he opens his empty mouth, and the words
cluster right where the lawyer puts them
I leaned on her face to stop her screaming –
like singing out *Amen!* to please the pastor,
like saying *I'm shit* to escape from the big guys
(words being light and slack as a string bag
shaped to whatever you want them to hold).

Or, being rare and rarely his own,
is it rather that words, once he hears himself speak them,
come to seem weighty and full of the truth?
Does he get to believe, for as long as he's talking,
that a girl screamed and he was the one who stopped her?
Does he imagine the press of her cheekbones?

Of course, in the nature of things, there's no knowing.
What's clear is he only half understands –
though he's learned the trick of seeming to, just by
repeating the words right after a person:
Yes, I waived my rights, and he's grinning
as if he's seeing himself in a motorcade,
while the jurors look grave, scribble on their notepads
the words that dance round his head like horseflies.

Sister Ship

On 6 March 1987, the passenger ferry, Herald of Free Enterprise, *capsized outside Zeebrugge, with the loss of 193 lives.*

1 *Relatives*

More than a month
they've swallowed strange food,
found patience, grateful phrases,
while gales poured havoc over her.

The town's familiar as a lifer's cell.
At night, they lie counting traffic lights,
brands of beer – unconnected things
to keep them even.

Not much to say;
just waiting, walking streets,
the dock, staring out there,
trying to, trying not to picture him.

Waiting for cranes to raise her,
for the sea to give him back
so they can all go home,
so they can sleep.

2 *Divers*

She's come to term,
a monstrous animal
slouched onto one side
for the delivery.

The sea sulks, stands off.
Tugs bob, useless,
while they, like puny midwives,
delve in her cluttered entrails

half-blind, grasping
a thigh, a shoe,
an arm stiff round a pillar,
easing it free,

171

becoming
instant mortuary professionals,
prepared for the look
of face after face, defaced.

3 *Afterwards*

The duchess came,
gave him a toy,
said, *Brave little boy.*

The prince came,
admired her curls,
said, *Brave little girl.*

The Minister came,
shook his hand,
talked of England.

The pop star came
with a TV van,
said, *Terrible, man!*

Reporters came,
said, *Tell about the horror.*
Look at the camera.

The ambassador came,
the nun and the police,
the doctor and the priest.

But Daddy didn't come,
Mummy didn't come,
his wife didn't come,

her husband didn't come,
their daughter didn't come,
their sons didn't come,

and night has come
like a black stone
in the throat.

4 *Sister Ship*

Months afterwards
we travel in the sister ship,
our luggage stuffed with images
made toy-like by the geometry
of page or screen.

What can we do with them?
We're bit players in a re-take
with an uneventful ending
turning the one before to history;

though you can sense her weight,
her three and more dimensions
as she slides seaward, slowly turns.

5 *Not us*

That evening,
when the shutting of bow doors
was left to enterprise
and enterprise was sleeping,
would it have been like this:

you and I
out on A deck, watching
receding lights
spangle the ink black,
when suddenly

the sky tips –
funny at first –
pressing us on the rail.
I have inflatable armbands
fit them on you –

or do I make
a bowline from my coat-belt –
either way,
as the surface rushes up
we grasp hands, jump, swim.

Or did it list to starboard?
We're thrown backwards
against an iron stair
we cling to, wedge ourselves
waiting for rescue.

Would it have been
like that? you and I
survivors? Always a way
for those who keep their heads,
those with enterprise?

6 *Cafeteria*

This ship is full of empty passengers,
a cargo of consumers. One could think
we are working our passage with our teeth,
biting, chewing, swallowing our way
from shore to shore.

                    The cafeteria
fills up at once, a patient, silent queue
intent on breakfast: piles of sausages,
tomatoes, baked beans, bacon, eggs, fried bread
and toast and marmalade;

                         as though we've been
invaded by those taken by the sea,
ravenous spirits thrown up in the wake.
We glut ourselves to fill a double void
with obvious comforts, never quite enough.

7 *Anniversary*

They look pinched by a wind
stronger than then
and colder.

They're quiet as they queue
to scatter wreaths and posies
on the water,

shifty sea
that swallowed flesh
as if entitled.

So much salt
our cheeks are stiff with it.

So much salt
our eyes are glazed with it.

The wind spits back
their tears for kin
man-slaughtered,

not mattering enough;
and no one saying sorry.
They're here as witnesses

for those more than fractions
of the one-nine-three,
the paper dead.

So much salt
our stomachs sicken of it.

So much salt
our tongues are raw with it.

They twist their grief into
flowers, cast them adrift.
Anger, more difficult to place.

Turning Point

You're standing in the supermarket queue
dreaming of difference;
or on a foreign street, you're weak
with possibilities there's no language for.
And you could walk
round the corner into that other place

but for the hours looping on themselves,
ordinary as knitting
you're too meshed in to see straight.
Each morning dazzles you with a tranche
of choices, distracting
from the sly way the needles skewer you.

Bad faith isn't high dramatic acts –
the Judas kiss, embezzlement –
it's allowing each innocuous stitch
to shift you from day to night
and back to day, no further on,
a little fitter for the shapeless droop

that lengthens to the final
casting off.
Out of what despair, or resolution,
might you refuse? And what
would guide you through
the chaos of your fraying ends?

Cutting Loose

At one time
at moments when the walls burst through the wallpaper
he could pause long enough
to slam the door behind him as he fled
into the hard-boiled street;
so that coming home, hours later, all was intact –
walls, clock, kettle
subdued to simple ticks and shrieks and silences.

Now the door stands gaping
as he hurtles out, in sight of the street's main chancers
and he knows his room will be
picked clean and pissed on (though not with particular malice).
But it seems immaterial,
a room in a film – and the thought is a sudden joy
and a clarification:
instead of a loop, his route will be straight forward.

His feet make jet-streams.
He rides in the bowl of his pelvis like a millionaire
and he sheds desire
for the squared-up scraps of lives in the lighted windows
as his leg-springs carry him
through streets speckled with the whites of eyes,
past Coke can and condom,
the newsprint beds of the rootless, birthday-less,

to the waste-ground
where gaunt backs of warehouses stand, guarded
by hogweed and sycamore.
And though he knows he's matter out of place,
a kind of dirt,
he's a giant under the sky, chewing nettles
like cheekfuls of bliss;
for now, breathing easily, at home.

Life in Tall Houses

So many years of the tall, smart
Happy Family museums
insulting us by their indifference to blinds;

blazing rooms, boasting
amply laid tables, modish clutter,
children playing chamber music;

bait, perhaps.

Years of impregnable locks
until we came to hunger more intensely
for those hugs, those conservatory flowers;

and the tall houses
cracked open like pomegranates
under the arithmetic of our desire;

a bit too easily.

The people sprang from their beds
with a curdled look, as though we
were what they'd always dreaded and needed.

The light inside the tall houses seems
misplaced, furniture paper-frail,
jasmine bent on dying.

We are left with a fistful of flies
and the thought of how the happy families
scattered into the city,

singing, or something like it.

Il Conto

You pay for the fifteenth-century palazzo.
You pay for three smiles in evening dress,
for just the right degree of deference.

You pay for the dexterity of wrists,
the flattering chorale of glass and silver;
for the proffered chair, flourished napery,

the snowy acres of the sommelier's waistcoat.
You pay for the plush hush of the ladies' room,
tiny tablets of geranium soap.

Pasta that leaves a coating on your teeth
is not, you tell yourself, the point. You pay
for the precision sprinkling of *parmigiano*,

for the slick ripple of Gershwin, the magnetism
of Fame and Money at the other tables,
for candle-flame that gilds you, draws you in.

You pay for your reflection in the window
where Dukes' mistresses once leaned. You pay
for a starring role in your own Sweet Life.

And you pay for the centuries-old tact
with which you're not pressed to a second course,
with which the *portiere* averts his eyes.

Tuesday at the Office

A human fly has climbed the pylon.
Stripped, but for shoes,
('I hope he gets sunburn,' Sandra says)
he's a cut-out against postcard blue.
We can't hear him, only see mimed anger
as he shouts down to firemen
perched on puny ladders, offering food.
('Waste of public money,' Sandra says)

It's like golf on TV.
We chat, type, photocopy,
looking up between jobs
at our man, monkeying about.
If he's going to jump, we want to see,
be made solemn, half hoping
it'll make sense of something.
('I know it's a cry for help, but,' Sandra says)

At some point, he's gone.
That night, we watch *Thames News*
to prove it happened, and we were there.
But there's no mention,
only traffic and a murder,
so he must have climbed quietly
back into his ordinary life.
('I knew he'd let us down,' says Sandra)

Wrong-footed

You're going down a long escalator
into the limbo of the Northern Line,
and despite all gratefully perceived distractions –
a fat balloon-seller gliding upwards,
Kew Gardens poster by a friend of yours –
you can see what's waiting at the bottom is
the subject of an undergraduate essay
you'd get a C for: weigh the respective claims
on the solitary coin that's in your pocket
of the flautist travestying *Summer Time*
and that grey bundle merging with the wall.
Giving to a busker is like shopping
(you're comfortable with that) paying for
a musical snack, instant insouciance;
it's something for something. She looks like your niece.
You don't want the despair of speechless begging
to chill your morning; that belongs outside
the world you think you live in, where one makes
an effort. So that when his body's angles
say life's shit-dark, and some twinge in your bones
says yes, you tell yourself that what you give
someone like that can never be enough,
or the right thing, that only love would do,
and what you've got is one coin in your pocket.
The unsolicited, junk notes sing
put it here...*the livin' is easy*. But you're thinking
maybe you shouldn't get by with a neat transaction;
this woman has her flute, and maybe smiles
into the mirror, liking the shape of her chin.
You want to turn and climb towards the light
but you know you'd only stay in the same place –
the thought from which the escalator trips you,
the essay in your head still at page one.

Blurred Vision

Out in the fast lane, life mimics
going places; no witnesses

to hands slithering on the wheel.
Tear vapour fogs the windscreen as,

on motorways to anywhere, men
cry in their private grief containers.

People they pass might be scandalised
by wide-open mouths boozily singing

but it's desperation unrefined
cracks such large holes in rigid faces.

Maybe they'd want to find themselves
in the hazy place before they were big boys;

but what they see is all one way,
mile upon mile of hard shoulder,

as they're driving, driving much too fast
to notice exits. Alone and dangerous.

Ourstory

Let us now praise women
with feet glass slippers wouldn't fit;

not the patient, nor even the embittered
ones who kept their place,

but awkward women, tenacious with truth,
whose elbows disposed of the impossible;

who split seams, who wouldn't wait,
take no, take sedatives;

who sang their own numbers, went uninsured,
knew best what they were missing.

Our misfit foremothers are joining forces
underground, their dusts mingling

breast-bone with scapula, forehead
with forehead. Their steady mass

bursts locks; lends a springing foot
to our vaulting into enormous rooms.

The Smell of Sweat

Sweat is our signature on air:
grapefruit, onions, Glenmorangie.

It is the first date,
the first exam, all firsts;

climb on the cliff path, straining
to work off a terminal prognosis;

rugby hugger-mugger, job well done,
the body throwing out exuberant salts;

nightmare-time – debt, the law,
ex-husband at the door;

one of lust's slippery bouquet
of juices; must of the prison cell.

Its traces swirl around us;
we draw daily breath

from this promiscuous reserve
of extreme moments, not knowing whose.

from

LOVE AND VARIATIONS

(2000)

Hands

(for Martin)

Five hundred miles
have wiped out the patterns
at your finger-ends,
the warm pockets of your palms.
I can't picture your hands

but I know they are
the bass line of a madrigal;
springboard that lets me go;
ample weight-bearing branches;
straight-furrowing plough.

Sometimes they look at each other –
don't they – and see
an insufficient thing.
But they're a Shaker rocking-chair,
beauty and use balancing.

They're a quilt that's right
for every season; deep box
of preserved fruits; my elbow room;
map of the awkward universe;
the sight of home.

My Wilderness

Landlocked, imagining licence to discover
the entire reach of you, island by island,
I think of early travellers. It wasn't men

whose medium was ink, paint or stone
who risked life for the literal, but those
who couldn't find a vessel for their dreams.

They would have started with prosaic tasks,
hustling and preparation; slipping out
in fair weather, prudently provisioned;

knowing where they were at first, then sailing
over the world's edge – though sea is sea,
its dangerous temperament at least familiar.

Wouldn't their hearts have thundered in their ribs
at the colossal cragginess of land,
fantasy, massed at the horizon's swell,

now irredeemably external?
What had kept them constant until then
was all they could envision but not yet touch:

all the sharp particulars of awe,
shimmering landscapes, demons and grotesques
that made the formed and formless *Wonderful.*

Hadn't they hoped to be transformed, until
imaginaries of ecstasy and fear
shrank, with the first scrape of keel on sand?

But as they opened up the wilderness –
staked out, mapped, collected, sketched – perhaps,
despite such rich empirical delights,

they paused to think how much more animate
had been their dream-creatures, their Fortunate Isles;
and found they couldn't quite remember them.

Recorded Delivery

I'll Show You My House

Don't bring politeness, just allowances.
Some of these objects stand outside taste.
They inhabit histories of love –

the pink chair, for instance,
insisting like a boil on being noticed;
though the two star hotel wallpaper,

the liquorice curtains winking and sneering
'wrong! wrong!' took me many hours
and twice as many dogged miles to find.

Your flawless eye is bound to see
the dross of accumulation like a thickening
around the waist. That's age for you.

Yes, it is always as tidy as this.
I haven't hidden - much. Here,
I'll fling open cupboard doors –

read the contents. Can you tell
how, for years, my affairs have been waiting
to be found in perfect order? I know which

three things I'd snatch if I had to run.
These are the bland and smiling rooms
of someone who's adept at surfaces.

Only – you should see my other rooms,
how cavernous they are, cobwebbed, cluttered;
ah, my invisible rooms are a different storey.

On Not Writing a Letter from Iona

When, after all those jolts and nearly lost connections,
you reach your island – mist, perhaps, swirling milk
along the shore – and you sit at the window, stillness settling
slowly, days stretched out before you like clean canvasses;

when you remember how, a world away, you said
'I'll write', said it deliberately yet, now, wonder
how you could have been so profligate;
know that I'll receive silence from you
as though it were a letter, and be glad, seeing
there can always be letters, while even small
stacks of days like clean canvasses are precious, few.

Semi-precious

You tell me about moonstones
chosen in India for someone else.
For yourself, a rope of coral.
No jewels for me – but on this page
you are giving me a gift of language,
restringing corals as they might be
the letters of my name; wearing me,
salt to salt, against your skin.

On Not Being Impulsive

Posting my letter through your door
I caught, through red stained glass, a sight
of you, back from your travels, reading
at the kitchen table; and it seemed right

that you should be roseate like that,
and I, seeing you - one glance all
I needed to preserve you: a glowing
lozenge in my nocturnal hall.

Ah, but I was tempted to knock,
being mad to hold you for a minute,
just that; to know your bone-and-muscle
realness, after so long; and hated it,

hated that this most natural thing
(just then, more longed for than any
words) would have been – wouldn't it? –
one knock, one hug, one minute too many.

Opal

You've given me all elements but one,
in this stone translated from its origins
to hang above my desk on a gold thread:
brilliant angelfish, oracle, drawn
from the dark reef of your duffle bag.

If we became less vivid to each other
it could turn filmy, like a dying eye.
But, then, would we care, or remember
that once it swung by a thread – fire, water, air –
into lamplight, into shadow?

'Are There Birds?'

The birds here are invisible to me,
flying on the safe side, in this country
where men shoot small birds for sport.

I hear them - cuckoo, finches' sweet
needle-point of sound, the sharp derision
of a woodpecker; and the nightingale's

nightly soliloquy in the sinister red prunus
whose leaves are being cast off - in May.
Superstitious, I want it to behave seasonably

but, much more, I want there to be
birds visible, to describe them to you;
vivid, remarkable ones, so you will come.

Since they're your natural kin - quick,
felicitous, conditioned not to trust - perhaps
they'll appear for you, settle near:

a palette of birds, an illuminated
library of feathered volumes
speaking for me. So you will stay.

Heartmarks

This frail-looking balustrade,
all that stood between us and certain
death on the paving-stones below,
is where we first touched without
a spun glass reticence between us.

That Soho market... this revolving door...
the layout of the city is peppered
with such places. To fix them
with precise coordinates of words
would arrest their gauzy meanings,

but on the map described by memory
you'll find me whirling nightly
from Bertaux to Pimlico, haunting
Long Acre, Kenwood, Gabriel's Wharf:
all the stations of love.

Boy with a Fish
(in memoriam SCM: 1944-1995)

1

For your funeral, we pin pictures of you
on a board. To revive you,

to assure ourselves light fell on you once,
smiler, joker. Blown egg.

Larking on a beach: cardboard playboy
in tilted Bogart panama, white twill;

the wedding (we're unsure, but choose it
for that flare of joy, part of the story).

No recent ones. Everyone stares hardest
at this one: aged fourteen, perhaps,

hefting an enormous bream you'd caught.
You look at us, hold out the fish,

shoulders hunched, offering.

2

Is that all – why aren't you top?
Father's bloodstock, his future winner.
He named his cabin-cruiser after you.

He shinned down the cliff of figures
like an alpinist. *See, it's easy!*
You, mute, swallowing his pride.

What did you take from your expensive schooling
but appearances? You couldn't allow
anyone to teach you anything. Never would.

Now, thinking of my rare, dutiful
enquiries from my side of the city,
I hear your cadence: *Nothing. Nobody.*

3

Come to clear the flat, we're clinging
to each other's common sense, to words
positioned carefully, like hand-holds.

The smell, a substance
invading even thought:
rotten food, unwashed skin.

Overwhelming waste. All furniture
engulfed by takeaways,
thousands of crushed tissues,

ruined clothes, three years'
newspapers, Marlboro packets, butts,
ash on ash on ash.

Only the telephone stands clear,
and beside it, placed, poems of mine
I don't know if you read.

This black bed, where they found you
comatose, blankets ravaged by mice
whose nests we startle: small, energetic lives.

Held in the light, even our most extreme
nightmares can become mere narratives.
There ought to have been words instead of this.

4

What draws tears isn't chaos,
but this mirror by the door
where you must have checked,
tidied your hair with this brush,
squared your shoulders, practised
that cellophane expression.
Then walked out to the street
and become invisible.

5

In masks and gloves,
like asbestos workers,
we bag up, bundle, scrub,
disinfect, retreating only
when dust grabs us by the throat.

Brutal, we pile stuff high in the yard,
call in the Council.
The house clearance man
offers twenty quid for everything.

Out go the ebony elephants,
a hundred unused guitar strings,
a lifetime's easy listening.

After three days, we have clean surfaces,
four stripped rooms, stinging with Dettol.

The estate agent talks prices. Talks *desirable*.

6

Your names were a three-piece suit.
The first, formal;
the second, father's heavy hand-me-down;

the surname, unusual, allowing
entry to the family romance:
the castle on the Borders.

You could have grown into it.
Father couldn't wait for that,
scornful when you tripped.

You learned a way of seeming,
tricked yourself out – elegance,
reckless generosity.

Time stained it. But it was
your last proud possession,
final covering.

7

How does a man get by with a skin too few?
He keeps very still,
so still, he can hear the surge of his blood as it travels;
so still, he discovers himself saying *no* in his sleep.

No attachment, no lurch of hope or ambition
leads him to reach out,
fearful of splits and cracks. Sensation is bandaged.
He treads with the delicacy of an acrobat

but attracts no admiring audience. He gathers himself
in a tatterdemalion rig-out –
habit, bravado, blind-alley facts – too ill-fitting
to keep out the cold. A garment that passes for skin.

8

Where did you put your self?

Not, lately, into work, though you had thrived
on office life, settled for peanut wages:
a tacit trade-off for the times you'd ring in
sick, or not turn up, after your benders.

Not into love. Was it belief in magic
(*gullible*, we reckoned, even then)
sent you spinning into marriage with
a girl you met in Tenerife? How soon

the disappointments mounted. Then she left,
taking the sapphire ring, the better linen,
draining your non-renewable resource
of confidence: *you're not a proper man.*

And not into these diaries: twenty years
of 'Mum rang', 'dentist', 'signed on', 'paid the gas',
what you ate, the occasional 'dirty evening'.
Where are you? In the silences.

9

I remember you new born,
a squashy thing between your legs –
something wrong!

Mother didn't put me right.
You were the son father longed for.
Later on, she'd say

you were too much like her,
as though some softness,
lack of drive, had been

passed down; no amount
of love enough to cancel out
her early luke-warm welcome.

Sitting with you those days of coma,
marking your laboured breath,
I see a wrong key in the wrong lock.

10

Scorpio. In mid-October,
you joked about the big Five-O –
bring on the zimmer frame – and talked
of *one or two odd jobs* around the flat
you never let us into. Sometimes,
I knew you were there, not answering.

That week at mother's, wanting the day
witnessed, you sounded bright, excited,
as though, at fifty, you'd be a man
of substance, with meaning in your wallet.

I don't know how it went. Soon, that place
received you back. So far beyond odd jobs.
Only five months for you to follow
your defeated fern, uncomplaining,
into the dark.

11

Love has struck me as a painful fact
I didn't know I knew. We couldn't cope
with saying it, but wrote, phrase-book fashion,
'Dearest S', 'Lots of...', 'XXX';
word packages we took care not to open.

What shocks me now is love's tenacity.
I think of the Rose of Jericho, its dour
tangle blossoming in rain. As strange,
after such stubborn drought, for the heart
to yield this piercing, anachronistic flower.

12

When she said, *It's all right, darling,*
everything's going to be all right now,
stroking your head, I'm certain
you heard her – the bone-familiar
voice that gave you birth, releasing you.

Poses, lies, bigotry, every awkward edge –
all your life's pitiful distractions –
slid from you then. In death, you became
more than material – pharoah, famine victim,
soldier, the dead, grey Christ. Every human.

Leasehold

Does everyone think this – one day I'll knock
at that childhood house, where trespassers now live,
and ask to see? But never do, shrinking
from too little, or too much, recall,
anxious to protect our box of shadows.

One winter evening, dressed in black,
I hitched open that same sticking gate
into the garden I'd not seen for decades.
Skirting the garage (no queasy Humber)
I came on the house, off guard and somnolent.

These were the dusk-colours of a photograph:
here I'd perfected the flip of stolen currants
from palm to mouth; and on that window-sill
risked a glassy death to read the night sky
for God's expression, his take on my fractured world.

Drawn to the one lighted window, I felt –
not nostalgia, it wasn't home I longed for
but for a second, reparative, twist
at turning points, the chance to etch a different
mark in that gas-fumed hallway, on those stairs.

*

Now, about to leave another house
on an open-ended journey, the idea,
departure, awes me – its solemnity,
and time leaching, making my skin prickle.
I try to hold it in a net of tasks.

Après moi... Lately, I dream I've come
back here to find doors hung on empty air,
rooms crumpled in on themselves
like toothless mouths. Stout walls pulverise
without my living life to nourish them.

I've occupied this chain of rooms as if
creating something permanent, the colours,
temperatures and light to love in, work in.
To be alone in – coming back at night
from the clamorous proximities of the city

to hear the door's sweet, self-sufficient click,
the healing silence. This is happiness:
a crowded tableful of friends I've brought
together, like the best ingredients, scatter,
talking still, into the street, and I

apply myself to the companionable
clutter – my order, my domain again.
And yet, the plumbing's gurgling irony
reminds me: the house is self-possessed.
Irrelevant, fastidious whites and ochres,

my gracefully shaped arch. Reversible.
The house, indifferent to taste, retains
its skeleton; and I, vain freeholder,
am little else but frivolous breath on glass,
the transient impress of foot and hand.

We're interchangable, we occupants.
In the small hours, sometimes boundaries slip.
A noise wakes you – a creaking joist, is it?
The springing of a catch? Silence. Then
someone's breathing somewhere in the room;

the walls are throbbing. Harsh, tense breaths
approaching very near. Dark is felt-thick;
You will yourself blockish as timber.
In those seconds, you travel a whole life-time
before you know the breathing as your own.

                              *

Lists, algorithms, long-term instructions,
all the will's scaffolding – as if sheer diligence
could painlessly tie up all ends and leave
no life-long conversations gaping
with all that's still to say, and won't be now.

Real time's run out; even a meta-list
won't hold me up. If I don't come back
they'll peel every room, skin by skin,
tissues of meaning loosened from their backing
to re-form, wander, settle where they can.

Will someone glance inside my notebooks?
All the lines and fragments – will they leap out
like clowns, assassins, suitors, militants?
Or, malnourished orphans, slip the page?
Words, the last skin; beyond them, nothing.

Les Autres *or* Mr Bleaney's Other Room

Hell is a hotel bedroom. Other people,
implicit in the trapped, pine-freshened air,
fill you with their discomforts – room not quite
warm enough, bed intolerant. It's clear

you're one of a sad company who've seen
themselves summed up by chintz and candlewick,
who've spat in this basin, interrogated this
same toilet bowl for signs; or, maybe, sick

of their own company, turned on TV
and tried to feel drama or panel game
might give a purchase on some richer life,
but found the room immured them just the same.

You, like them, lie squeamish on the sheet
that veils the map of other people's lust,
fever, clumsiness, incontinence;
toss, sleepless and resentful, under musty

blankets' meagre weight, and realise
how you have buttressed your identity
with fragile props, convinced yourself of your
uniqueness. Foolish. You'll see – when you die

you'll land up in the final hotel bedroom,
where your mucus, dandruff, pubic hairs and sweat
will (but for the finer print of DNA)
turn out to be like anyone's you've met;

and though to swallow your disgust and breathe
deeply the air you share with everyone,
as if you loved them, might transform a hell
into a kind of heaven – can it be done?

Leaving Present

The ritual clock: you've done your time,
now's the time for the time of your life,
for all the time in the world. You place
the clock where it can see you.

Time's always come in blocks. Now
it floods the landscape of your days,
effacing the old boundaries.
Your purposes dissolve in it.

Time keeping's as unnecessary
as you are, but you're shackled to
this bland-faced border-guard,
its smug and vacuous syllabics

prophesying mean time,
injury time, time out of mind,
the moment when your time
is up, is up, is up.

The Woman Next Door

(for Susan Wicks)

At 3 a.m., the sky rips open; fury
beats on the slates, hammers the windows.
The drains gag on excess.

Wind, shrieking in a foreign language,
jackboots the door, beside itself;
lightning searches every corner.

I know my neighbour's roof leaks,
that she must be madly juggling
with bowls; deprived of sleep.

I tuck the duvet round me.
The rain is being hurled
by some unreasoning power.

She should have had it fixed.
She's like that. We each have a phone.
I have a spare bed. She's probably

shifting to the dry side of hers,
clinging to the edge...
Broom, yellow plastic dustpan,

float, clatter against furniture.
The water rises, lifts her, hurtles her
out, over the drowned garden,

down to the valley bottom,
where the road's a river;
and I spot her, in the sensible

pyjamas I've seen on the line,
rotating, tossing like a log, until
she's swept into the woods,

and I lose her...At 10 a.m.,
her curtains are still closed.
I sit on the terrace

in rinsed pearl light,
eating fresh bread, reading
that book by Eva Fogelman.

The Jew of Chantérac

Back then, no one would have called him that. No feature, no practice,
no seven-branched candlestick, no distinctiveness marked him,
not even his name – not Lévi but Demartin, not Mordecai but Jacques.

Did someone with a gun at their throat, and a son in the Maquis, seize
a wisp of hope – as one might try to soft-soap an ordinary bully,
as *I'll take you to where there are otters,* or something else rare and harmless?

Or, out of no special grievance, no previous sense of difference,
into the mouth of some citizen who'd always been anxious to please
and couldn't stop now; or into a mind sharp for self-advancement

sprang Jacques, his name already a tempting sop to throw
the Gauleiter, who snapped him up, although demanding
tribute more abundant than a single, peaceable Jew.

But later, no one wanted to rake over who'd said what;
and because the white-veiled girls were shut up in the church and burned;
and the boys in their Sunday clothes were rounded up and shot

he hardly counts. So although each year, even now, people
cram into the church to honour the names of those who could have been
more to them, teenage great-uncles and aunts, there's no memorial

to the man in the cobbler's shop who turned out to be a Jew,
to the way they shouted and spat; to the ancient sway of his back
as he stuffed things into a case, enough for a week or two.

What remained of him after he'd gone north-east up the narrow-gauge track?
An increasingly abstract guilt in some elderly breast? Vague stories.
A small gap: there's never since been a Jew in Chantérac.

Sunset Over Tottenham Hale

Gospel Oak to Barking, Barking to Gospel Oak:
the usual pleasures of the grubby train that shuffles
me to work and back include sinful snacks

novels in day-time. But not the raw
heaps of graveyard steel, urban farm
where everything moults in despair.

Nor terrace fronts whose every brick
is picked out in shaky black, or encrusted
from ground to eaves in multi-coloured mosaic.

My throat aches at the patience of it;
I think of my own, equally convinced, aesthetic.
Then, today, nature took sides and elected kitsch

throwing a vast canopy of flamy tatters
over the flatlands of east London. Brick,
glass, concrete reflected glory; altostratus

streaming in Strictly Ballroom rose,
Cartland mauve, Metro Goldwyn carmine
and russet – a brash brass band of a blaze.

At first, no one looked, but stared stiffly
at newspapers, slumped as if too full
of trouble to be touched; or as if

every day, Canary Wharf stood like a survivor
of *blitzkrieg,* and the sky spread out such gifts.
But then first one face then others came alive,

smiles passed between us as a flood
of copper, spilling across the reservoirs,
transformed greasy grey to dragon's blood.

The Life and Life of Henrietta Lacks

That was me in the New Look
sassy as hell, in the days
when wicked was wicked;
not the fist on hip of a woman
who knows she's cooking
a time bomb tumour;

not a number's up smile
like a dame who figures
she'll not be getting the wear
from all those yards
of cloth she scrimped for,
who'll be dead at thirty.

Dead? For forty years
my cloned cervical cells
have had a ball in Petri dishes
gorging placenta soup,
multiplying like their crazy mother –
the first ever cell line,

flung like spider's thread
across continents I never got to visit,
the stuff of profits, reputations
from Melbourne to Baltimore;
hot property, burning mindless
energy I'd have known how to use.

They never asked. Never said
How's about you live for ever,
like immortal yogurt? I'm bought,
sold like cooking fat. But I get even,
grow where I'm not supposed,
screw up experiments.

Soon, they'll have the know-how
to rebuild me from a single cell.
A rope of doubles could jitterbug
from here to Jupiter. Meantime,
I'm grabbing my piece of the action,
hungry to cry my first cry again.

The Front

In old age, when the land begins to tilt, they roll
like marbles, gently, towards the coast, coming to rest
in condominiums with impatient gardens, and rules.

Here, washing lines, ragged cries of pain
are unacceptable. Here are brave faces, a glaze
of gentle manners. The past curls up behind them.

Promenade punctuates their mornings, those aches
affirming one's still there. They step out,
troupers, earning the comfort of hot chocolate,

fighting to hold the line against decay with camouflage,
cunning, with not naming parts that can't be helped.
They can dance, can swing an iron, and are doing it

for all of us – up ahead, acting impervious
to tides and weather, to show how one can smile
beside that slippery remembrancer, the sea.

Freedom of the City

Office blocks like silver-suited posers
are mirrors for each other. All day, weather
glides across their beautiful, blank faces.

Below, you scurry in pursuit of choices –
this film or that, what kind of food, which jacket
will suit you best, and is it still in fashion?

And underlying those, the other questions –
how are you doing, where is it you're heading,
who will you be today? For you are never

your own whole story. It doesn't take some clever
dick in the Sorbonne to show you what
a circus of selves you are. It's a pleasure

to give them an airing, since you have the leisure
to be *flâneuse*, mark, rent-a-crowd...though thinking,
as you drop a coin in some young man's guitar case –

is his face, turned blankly to yours, is your face
so different, after all, from what's above:
the play of surface on another surface?

Birthmark

Sun throws my shadow onto the stone bench
and within it are lichens: ashy green, ochre,
scabby home to blood red micro-beetles.

Insistence, grip, their greed for *lebensraum*
have mapped this sandstone with a pointillist
scatter of colonies, macular settlements

draining colour from their hinterland:
these, the townships of Natal, and these
the farms and homesteads of my ex-pat uncles.

My silhouette incorporates them.
They make me sin ugly, give me features
I shall own, until cloud erases me.

The Blessing

(for Sidney Buckland)

Suddenly
a flying pair of compasses
described desperate parabolas
through the room,
buffeting bookcases,
scrabbling for purchase,
terror terrified.

A rush of purpose, then,
arrowed it for sunlight,
dashed it against
the puzzle of unyielding air
to a stunned thump on the floor.

I took it outside,
folded its rumpled wings.
It was still. But blinked, blinked,
as if to reassess a world
where matter could be this deceitful.

Such nearness was peculiar.
I stroked its back
with a slow, humming finger.
It cocked its head,
looked left, right, then
launched off;
instantly, just one more sky diver.

Might it not carry, though,
some organic trace
of being comforted –
as I will, of being
shaken by frantic flight;
palpitating blue?

Spring Offensive

May's the month for optimistic acts:
seedlings – pansies, stocks, geraniums –
bedded in, gauche first-day-at-schoolers.
Your thumbs have blessed them, inner eye furnishing
dowdy beds with dazzling coverlets.

Through the lengthening dusk, snail battalions
creep on prehensile bellies from their dugouts.
They bivouac around your bright hopes,
slurp rich juices; vandal lace-makers
growing fat on your would-be colours.

You stumble out at dawn and catch them at it,
scrawling silver sneers on wall and path,
and snatch them from their twigs, impervious to
their endearing horns, their picture-bookness.
You crush them, or worse, lay down poisonous snacks.

Yet aren't their shells as lovely as petunias,
patterned like ceramic works of art
from a more coherent age? And might they not
defend with slow, tenacious argument
their offspring, soon to fizz and drown in salt?

Summer's on their side. Each night, new recruits
will graduate from dark academies.
You lie plotting extravagant revenges.
Asleep, you're in a world where, very slowly,
children, friends, are running out of air.

Pentecost

A constant tumble downstream
presses through a slight narrowing
and produces not steady sound
but an altercation between water
and water, water and stone.
Gulping laughter as the river
clears its throat and passes on,
slipping through watercresses
that resist what must be,
this perpetual escape,
as if drenched in such fixed nostalgia
they can't welcome the continual new.

A storm rising, and the field of rye,
knowing and not knowing,
stands en bloc, until the wind
gathers itself into a passion,
sweeps among the standing stalks
stirring, harrassing them all ways
until the whole charged field
is a pan of roiling green;
or a palimpsest, bearing
every version of the wind's
rage for expression;
while each plant flexes, weathering.

But it ends like this:
after a day of busyness,
when it has rained, but stopped at last,
and the earth exhales pleasurable breath
at the sun's late reappearance,
two blackbirds release joyful voices
in endlessly inventive antiphons;
praise singers, offering up a line,
catching, re-forming it. And this is
what should be – unconfined ambition,
raising above the stream
a shining ziggurat of sound.

By the Time You Read This

She's lost her touch with doors –
push or pull almost always wrong.
By such improbabilities, a person
comes to feel chosen for punishment.

Old age must be like this – no point,
walking on stranger's feet,
drawn to the centre of the earth.
Her cheek thumps the pavement.

This is an old sin with a neutral name.
Objects treat her as the enemy she is;
cartons impregnable, taps unyielding,
needle's eye closed against her thread.

*

The scales are constant
but she's become micro-thin,

contained between
two faces of the page.

People write on both sides of her,
the smooth and the smooth;

they think they're
making an impression.

In another room,
a woman is screaming.

Uselessly carrying on.

*

Remember me.

I am marcasite for mother's finger,
father's enamelled trophy.

I am a gleaner of abandoned shells
wasting for the rinse of sea.

I am a picture in an exhibition
by blind photographers.

I am a deaf-mute harnessing vibrations
in a pail of pitch.

I am a masked crab. Dismember me —
discover a cache of shreds.

The Perversity of Mirrors

You could spend years of waking hours in front of them
and not catch how, nor exactly when
three-dimensional geometry goes soft on you:
features drawn on a slow-punctured balloon.

Since flesh will never re-compose itself
you want to splash your eyes with indigo,
gloss your teeth fluorescent, your life
made over in epileptic stripes.

Once, I told a man whom I respected
I'd refurbished my house all pink and green
with mirrors everywhere, while I
kept to myself washed terra cotta,

aquamarine, uncluttered walls
in the house he'd never visit – hoping
he'd see through me, such a talent
being part of what I loved in him.

I still regret the throw-away vulgarity
that lodged ugly rooms in his mind's cellar
where I'm mirrored, fairground foolish,
having no hold on what is beautiful.

Missing You

That you had that smile we'll all remember,
that you had the perfect voice for Gershwin,
that your children are, of course, a credit,
that your wife stands here taut-lipped and tearful

makes the vicar's work easy as he re-frames you
as a deft montage, our take-home present.
Your coffin stands trestled at the altar – and you,
already you're mist, missing in translation.

Yes, you were strong in the defence of dolphins,
but are you content in your padded coat of epithets?
Or will you come to me wearing that other smile
with the thirty-two-in-one wicked meanings?

Sitting for Manou

Manou is doing my portrait in gouache.
We're in her high studio with the unkind glare,
massed with the prints she sells; her paintings
like jewels, like electricity. As she positions me,

I wonder – how can I, neat and beige
and common as a glove, be transposed
into that intensity. But she is responsible.
She narrows her eyes to shut me in.

Her ritual passes at the canvas,
fencing footwork, her urgent muttering,
are crystallised desire. She makes herself
the channel for what I am, what I am not.

The space between us shimmers like hot tar;
seeing, being seen, a circuit I long to escape
to somewhere safer. But I've signed up
for malaise, this active stillness.

Am I these colours, planes, surfaces?
She labours to bring me to light.
I submit to the uncomfortable squeeze
of being remoulded; and attend the birth.

Two Quiet Women

Kate P gets into Balliol.
Her friend, Nicole,
who's always been considered dim,
gets in nowhere. Aimless, glum,
she moves to Headington.

Kate's crushed by ex-Etonians,
the way they walk,
the grown-up-baby way they talk.
She dreads tutorials, is getting
phobic about writing,

thinks of suicide. But wait,
it's not too late.
Each week, she and Nicole read,
discuss, then, when they're agreed,
Nicole writes the essay.

Kate's tutor says he is impressed,
although he finds
in between, he can't call her to mind.
Nicole dons subfusc, goes to Schools,
sits Kate's Finals.

Kate gets a starred First. Nicole,
by deed poll,
changes her name to Katherine P.
Kate and Kate, with their degree,
are hot property.

One quiet woman is much like another.
Two quiet women can take on the world and his brother.

Undine

Come to me, husband, beautiful stupid one, satin-skinned handful;
goat-leap the coast path as though you were running to meet the applause
of ten thousand admirers. I've watched you until it's no longer a pleasure.

Come to my cave. The eddies are sucking on nothing but foretaste
of you, sweet frigate. Now you, too, are wet as the sea, and as eloquent;
cries flood your throat like the rasp and thrash of incoming rollers.

*

I've swallowed you into my future through all my insatiable mouths –
unbearable if you had left as though this were some everyday dalliance,
carelessly vaulting the breakwaters, whistling, smelling of salt.

*

The tide has retreated; the sand is a frowning expanse in the semi-light.
Gulls wheel and seek; their mewling a restless complaint, out of tune
with the listless slap, the sullen, reproachful sigh of the sea.

My love, my bridge to the world of steel cities, of dancing and flight –
why is there pain when I think what I did to you? Why do my eyes stream
feeling your monstrous child swim in me, vigorous, mortal as fish?

Constanze's Wedding

(for Gregory Warren Wilson)

1

He insisted, not wanting me to take it from politeness:
if I didn't like it – meaning more than like – I should be honest.
I would have been (we have that much easiness between us)
but how would I not love such mouth-watering blue, the mystery
of how the flowers are made, felicities of glass, chased silver?

Later, he told me how, in his Venice room, he'd tried it on,
stared in the mirror to judge if I'd like it, see as he did.
I understood. Every morning I try on my whole body,
dress myself in desire; and he's the mirror, the appraising
eye that sees me, deficient past disguising. Today

when my longing, finally unchecked, will take me to the door
where this beginning ends, what will he make of me? Will he see
what it takes to bring him a gift pierced through with such misgiving?
I'll wear his necklace. They say Venetian glass splits, shivers
when danger touches it. If he doesn't like me, will it know?

2

Afterwards, it was as if a carp, too big
for its bowl, threshed this way and that
inside my head. The night turned to marble,
moonlight drained colour from the counterpane.

Had he called me beautiful, I'd have shrunk away
(the ugly sister has the thinnest skin) but once
I'd seen him take up a neglected viola
and felt I understood its joy in realising

its full register, the voice he knew was there.
Now I know I had hoped too specifically.
There was so much I didn't understand
and he said nothing to tell me if I pleased him

so that, after he slept, my body was the hollow
of the bell clanging each quarter; the rumpled linen,
dry cliffs ranged between us, until I heard him
sing in his sleep: *Ach ich liebte, war so glücklich!*

It's Not the Same

If I say *I love you,* it is not the same
as if you say it.

A pair of Tories cast non-identical votes.
Two ten-year-olds don't murder the same toddler.

Two athletes do not fail the same drugs test.
We each die of a unique disease.

My parents did not live in the same marriage,
swallowed different silent Sunday roasts.

When we share a Granny Smith, you see red,
though we may never know this.

Since last week's cool is this week's boring;
because words are mercury, not bricks;

because a flip remark can change the world;
and the mind is always fidgeting with its own furniture,

you never step into the same jeans twice,
nor out of the same bed, nor into the same poem;

you never play the same favourite track twice,
nor speak the same platitude.

And when I said *I love you,* yesterday,
I meant 'I can feel your attention wandering';

when I say it tomorrow, I may mean,
'I want to see if I believe it when I hear it.'

But today, *I love you* is as almost simple,
is as nearly literal as you'll ever get.

Jacques Lacan's Table

My table pretends it's solid,
that it's the same table now as yesterday,
that it exists, when I'm not sitting at it.

Once, it shuffled over to the glass
and saw such robust lines and angles,
such harmonies, coherence of design

that it's not been happy since, yearns
for that immaculate, whole tablehood,
transcendence of the quaking flux

of molecules, kaleidoscopic selves,
surface barely able to contain
dizzy plurality.

It seeks comfort from accomplices,
is grateful for a touch of beeswax,
gives me back the image of my hand.

It suits me to collude,
so I load it with books, a pot of coffee,
lean my elbow on it, doing this.

Love and Variations

Love. No one asked me for it.
No one's fault if hearing
that way of saying 'know',
black ink on thick cream paper,
the scent of crushed gum leaves,
bring this vertigo.

*

It's like childbirth,
self-inflicted; the way
you let yourself fall;
new life stirring you
to one-track smiles;
the resolve, this time,
to do it differently;
the way, every time,
you forget how it hurts.

*

I have neuralgia. Or is it?
Restless legs, blurred vision.
At the sound of the telephone
I sweat sheets of ice.
My doctor, sceptical, makes
an ayurvedic pulse diagnosis.
Love, she says. In the circumstances,
an absurd complaint. Not contagious.

*

This is the fictional house
I've chosen: locked closets,
lovely rooms pleasuring themselves.
Narrow ledges where I try to settle.
I wander among shifting screens
I'd thought were walls, and am lost.

*

Love is *scordatura*;
a cello forgetting itself,
entranced by wilder possibilities;
a C string, insanely

relinquishing its proper pitch.
It is joy breaking into a run
despite the habit of caution,
despite the fault line in the bone.

*

If love's the theme, in the first variation
I'm tuned at awkward intervals;

in the second, I'm playing the wrong part;
we've forgotten all the notes in the third;

but in the fourth we remember, and then
our skins sing like a choir of wine glasses.

*

Sometimes, thinking of him,
I see a hare – not one puppeted
by the somersaults of Spring,
but a hare in Summer, power embodied,

made for *grands jetés*, delighting;
now tensed against incursion, now
tacking away, embroidering the field
free-style, because it must.

*

Far from the indifferent North,
my love and fury flourish
in the self-same southern latitude.
Out of the stuff of longing they give
birth to themselves in different writing;
but would he understand how
inseparable they are, my siamese twins
love and rage, joined at the heart?

*

How can the woman who loves
and the woman who writes poems about it
and the woman who writes about writing
about loving someone who might be him
walk the same wire together?

*

I won't give them up,
the thoughts he finds 'too much',
strings slung across absences.

But the gods have chosen him
to teach me paradox: already
I've let go what I never had.

Soon, feckless as a thrush, and as repetitive,
I'll perch so lightly in his branches
my song won't agitate a single leaf.

*

When he's exhausted, I want to author his sleep,
build a perfectly shaped stanza for him to rest in.
Don't tell me – I know the avarice of giving;
how even a baby sleeps its own sleep entirely.
I used to fidget round my unconscious child,
sing within earshot, greedy to be necessary again.

*

We're dancing a tango.
    I'm coming to trust
        his pace, his distance
            from the vertical.

            At this angle, nothing for it
                but to give myself
                    to the invention
                        uncertainty releases:

                        dialect we forge
                            from closeness, breaks;
                                hieroglyphs
                                    on earth and air.

                        And what can be said
                            isn't the half of it.

*

All that turbulence,
the prickling static
of old clingy habits;

all those high-priced,
uncomfortable garments
I've thought were love.

On a long out-breath,
one by one by one,
I let them drop.

They creep back, of course,
over my chest, solar plexus.
I'm patient with them,

knowing how it is;
breathe out, let them
fall away again. Again.

Only then, uncovered,
can I begin to call things
by their proper names.

*

Love: a clear pool, a kingfisher
flashing across, reflected.

Once seen, the kingfisher can't be un-seen —
it blesses the inward eye perpetually.

It may be rare, elusive. It may
prize the free air above everything.

But water holds awareness of the grace,
the brilliance, and is changed for good.

NOTES

Varanasi: Varanasi, formerly known as Benares, is the city on the Ganges to which, traditionally, Hindus wish their ashes to be brought after death.

Reflections on Glass: Glass is classified as a liquid (a) because of the way it behaves. Whereas a sold melts suddenly when heated, a liquid changes imperceptibly as the temperature rises. (b) At the atomic level, the atoms of a solid are arranged in a patterned way. In a liquid they are disorderly. So it is with glass.

Life Time: The epigraph, *'Es ist der alte Bund'* (It is the ancient bond) is a line from the cantata entitled *Gottes Zeit ist die allerbeste Zeit* (Actus Tragicus), which is concerned with death and hope. The German word 'Bund' carries a similar range of meanings, and has the same root, as the English 'bind', 'bond' and 'band'. 'I shall die, but that is all that I shall do for death', is a line from 'Conscientious Objector', by Edna St Vincent Millay.

Facing Magritte: Based on Magritte's painting, *Attempting the Impossible*, which portrays a painter bringing into being not a picture of a woman, but the woman herself.

Woman Pursued by Dragon Flees into the Desert: This is the subject of a stained glass window in the Sainte Chapelle, Paris.

Death of a Dancer: *Prosecco:* a sparkling wine drunk as an aperitif.

Lust in Translation: *Le néant* = nothingness.

Playing with Words at Abu Ghraib: Abu Ghraib is the prison in Iraq where torture and humiliation of Iraqi prisoners was freely practised by US military personnel, following the invasion in 2003.

Woman Bathing in a Stream: Rembrandt: This painting is in the National Gallery in London

The Balcony: This painting is in the Musée du Jeu de Paume, Paris.

Les Autres *or* Mr Bleaney's Other Room: *'L'enfer, c'est les autres'* (hell is other people) is a line from Sartre's play *Huis Clos*. The poem follows the metrical pattern of Philip Larkin's 'Mr Bleaney's Room'.

The Woman Next Door: Eva Fogelman: *Conscience and Courage: Rescuers of Jews during the Holocaust* (Victor Gollancz, 1995).

The Life and Life of Henrietta Lacks: Henrietta Lacks died in 1951, but her cells, amounting to several times her original weight, live on in laboratories around the world.

Undine: Undine, spirit of the waters, was created without a soul. By marrying a mortal and bearing his child she acquired a soul and, thereby, a sense of right and wrong.

Constanze's Wedding: *Oh I loved, I was so happy!*, sung by Constanze in *Die Entführung aus dem Serail*, written in the year of Mozart's marriage to Constanze Weber.

Jacques Lacan's Table: Lacan, French psychoanalyst, originated the concept of the 'mirror stage' of child development.

Love and Variations: *scordatura* is the abnormal tuning of a stringed instrument, e.g. for the purpose of increasing the compass.

Index of titles and first lines

Poem titles are shown in roman type, sequences in bold italics, first lines (some abbreviated) in italics.

A constant tumble downstream, 211
Afterwards, 172
A good lie's an achievement, like tightrope walking, 58
A human fly has climbed the pylon, 180
Adam said to Eve, a bit down-hearted, 50
Advent in Bratislava, 1992, 165
After he's gone, 39
All day I sit cross-legged with the women, 84
All the savannah-sultry afternoon, 45
All those names mangled on Ellis Island, 60
America, 168
Among the other things, 24
Anna, 122
Ankle Straps, 47
Anniversary, 174
'Are There Birds', 190
At best, there's heart in it, and fire, 26
At one time, 177
At the Edge, 55
At the start of summer, as every year, 22
At 3 a.m, the sky rips open; fury, 202

Back then, no one would have called him that. No feature, no practice, 203
Balancing Accounts, 95
Ballade, 65
Beauty's Not a Word They'd Needed Much, 56
Because a bit of colour is a public service, 126
Before, this box contained my mother, 146
Between croissants and croque monsieur, 106
Between the Lines, 71
Birth Rite, 112
Birthmark, 208
Blessing, 83
Blurred Vision, 182
Boy with a Fish, 192
Brave face, 39
Broken Moon, 81
By the Time You Read This, 212

Cabaret Song, 52
Cafeteria, 174
Call it hazing, 62
Can you imagine this, 150
Cancelling the deathbed scene, 43
Changing the Subject, 118
Chesil Beach, 18
Choosing the Furniture, 125
Christ, in his private ecstasy of pain, 87
Christmas Circulars, 117

Class is irrelevant in here, 122
Coat for an Undergraduate, 147
Come to me husband, beautiful stupid one, satin-skinned handful, 218
Community Care, 57
Confidence, 58
Constanze's Wedding, 219
Creation might have been like this, 143
Crocheted, 91
Crossing the Border, 162
Curtains, 91
Cutting Loose, 177

Day Trip, 90
Dear Departed, 13
Dearest, what do you mean?, 48
Death of a Dancer, 36
Death Speaks After the Tone, 155
Diagnosis, 119
Difficult Passages, 124
Divers, 171
Does everyone think this – one day I'll knock, 198
Don't bring politeness, just allowances, 188
Driving Through France, 106
Driving to meet you, 158
Duende, 67
Dusk, and the boathouse keeper, 17

Embroidery, 84
Envoi, 88
Erdywurble, 77
Even the day, 41
Explaining Zero Sum from the Snowdrop Hotel, 68
Exposure, 33

Fable, 54
Facing Magritte, 34
Family Planning, 92
File Past, 148
Fish, 85
Five hundred miles, 186
For weeks he worked to clear his ground, 56
For your funeral, we pin pictures of you, 192
Forty years this month, 130
Freedom of the City, 207
From Italy, by way of Harrods, 147
From Rosa in São Martinho, 83
Für Therese, 133
Futures, 85

Getting There, 80
Ghost Stations, 138
Gifts, 152
Girls Awake, Asleep, 115
Girls, dressed for dancing, 116
Give Me a Piece of Your Mind, Fat Man, 66
Going up the Line: Flanders, 102
Gospel Oak to Barking, Barking to Gospel Oak, 204
Graffiti, 104

Hands, 186
Hands off, 42
He asks her to promise she'd let him know if she were dying, 43
He insisted, not wanting me to take it from politeness, 219
He used arrive without no warnin', 96
He was a gloss on that English garden of roses, 159
He was good at telling, 119
Heartmarks, 191
Hell is a hotel bedroom. Other people, 200
Here is my clutch of humbugs, fickle honey bees, 92
Hours later, it seems, the pigeons are still wheeling, 36
How Are You?, 121
How I Altered History, 53

I have inherited another woman's flowers, 120
'I haven't seen you, love.' She means it kindly, 57
I Shall Paint My Nails Red, 126
I want to feel my bones packed snug in their upholstery, 66
If, by now, we have the faces we deserve, 21
If I say I love you, it is not the same, 220
If I should start to think too vividly, 93
Il Conto, 179
I'll Show You My House, 188
I'll tell you why, 133
I'm brilliant at clearing my cupboards of clutter, 52
I'm on a day trip to our shared frontier, 128
I'm sophisticated in my Cuban heels, 76
I'm spun through time widdershins, 110
I'm walking into La Porchetta, 156
Immigrants, 60
In her dream, she doesn't know who, 43
In my fiftieth year, 126
In old age, when the land begins to tilt, they roll, 206
In this garden, after a day of rain, 157
In-Patient, 120
Intensive Care, 79
InterCity, 108

Interminable nights, 41
Is there no answer to sexual obsession, 97
It started with my grandmother, 118
It was always said – she, 131
It was slippery blind surfaces, 144
It's all in the seeing, 39
It's Not the Same, 220
I've hung the washing out, 124

Jackets are easy; even the dashing scarves, 14
Jacques Lacan's Table, 221
Jealousy, 441
Just 'woman', 113

Kate P gets into Balliol, 217
Knowing Our Place, 122

La Dame à la Licorne, 32
Landlocked, imagining licence to discover, 187
Leasehold, 198
Leaving Present, 201
Les Autres *or* Mr Bleaney's Other Room, 200
Lessons in Air Kissing, 24
Let us now praise women, 183
Letter from Szechuan, 94
Life and death in another room, 43
Life in Tall Houses, 178
Life Time, 30
like a cat hunched before a cupboard, 27
Longing for some thing to be different, 28
Looking for myself, 132
Looping the coast, 83
Love and Variations, 222
Love is water, over shared history, stone, 18
Love. No one asked me for it, 222
Lust in Translation, 49

Manou is doing my portrait in gouache, 216
May's the month for optimistic acts, 210
Missing You, 215
Mme Verklaede, mother of four tall sons, 102
Moment, 158
Months afterwards, 173
More than a month, 171
Mother's Girl, 82
Mouthfuls, 75
My day is fettered by my mother's steps, 89
My father's parents sold fish, 77
My First Cup of Coffee, 76
My Life as a Green-lipped Mussel, 21
My niece walks with me in moonlight, 85
My table pretends it's solid, 221
My Wilderness, 187

Night Harvest, 140
No real men here, 84
Not the place I fled from, 83

Not Us, 173

Office blocks like silver-suited posers, 207
On Not Being a Nature Poet, 109
On Not Being Impulsive, 189
On Not Going Anywhere, 48
On Not Writing a Letter from Iona, 188
On the Map, 64
One, 160
Opal, 190
Opposite me, 108
Orphanage, 87
Our land has forgotten the taste of rain, 100
Our Peacock, 159
Ourstory, 183
Out in the fast lane, life mimics, 182
Out of range, 43
Out of Reach, 161
Out-Patients, 118
Outside, 124

Paper having acquired a poor image, 104
Partners, 131
Patching, 84
Passed On, 146
Pentecost, 211
Personal Effects, 13
Photograph, 86
Piccadilly Line, 116
Picking up a small white feather, 109
Pictograph in Dust, 100
Playing with Words at Abu Ghraib, 62
Poppies, 96
Postcard, 83
Posting my letter through your door, 189
Presents for Duncan, 154
Procession, 87
Prognoses, 78

Raja...puja..., 161
Recorded Delivery, 188
Reflections, 132
Reflections on Glass, 29
Relatives, 171
Reserve, 41
Rough crossing, 40
Ruby Wedding, 130

Sathyaji, 17
Semi-precious, 189
She counts the years and months it went on before they parted, 43
She gives him – things. They're paradoxical, 41
She read about the grape diet, 38
She remembers a mother waving from a train, 82
She'd always loved the word, 35
She'll try to be the just good friend, 42

'She'll walk something like this...', 78
She's come to term, 171
She's lost her touch with doors, 212
She's packed, 95
Shoes, 14
Shouting, they heave the dead weights, 85
Showing, 111
Sign, 41
Since I've not known another birth, 112
Sister Ship, 171
Sister Ship, 173
Sitting for Manou, 216
Skin Distance, 150
Sliced flat, androgynous, 151
Small again, I was pitting my mute will, 166
So many years of the tall, smart, 178
So that's who she was, 86
Sports Day, Miss Cook, 80
Spring Offensive, 210
Strawberries, 110
Striking Distance, 164
Suddenly, 209
Sun throws my shadow onto the stone bench, 208
Sunset Over Tottenham Hale, 204
Sweat is our signature on air, 184

Ten days to New Year, the fog's cold comfort, 165
Ten years ago, I could have brought a book, 154
Thanatos, 166
That evening, 173
That great operatic bunch of tulips you bought on impulse, 67
That was a haloed sound, 168
That was me in the New Look, 205
That you had that smile we'll all remember, 215
The Arc de Triomphe Looks Defeated, 46
The Archbishop and the Cardinal, 99
The Balcony, 114
The Bed, 129
The big, beautiful copper-haired, 120
The birds here are invisible to me, 190
The Blessing, 209
The Chairman's Birthday, 136
The curtains said, 125
The day before, my father, 136
The duchess came, 172
The engine throbs, 88
The Fall, 145
The Front, 206
The Jew of Chantérac, 203
The leaning tower of lemons, 39
The Life and Life of Henrietta Lacks, 205
...the motorway starts here – the thick red line, 64
The Oldest Story, 50
The Other Woman, 39

The Perversity of Mirrors, 214
The Power of Prayer, 38
The reassurance of the frame is flexible, 103
The Redness of Poetry, 26
The rest of your life starts, 145
The ritual clock: you've done your time, 201
The Silence of the Lions, 45
The Smell of Sweat, 184
The Trial of Lyman Atkins, 170
The Uncertainty of the Poet, 97
The way it stands against the dark, 25
The Way We Live Now, 156
The White Room, 28
The Woman Next Door, 202
The Wood Turner of Jaubertie, 22
The Word, 118
Then, somewhere over Greenland, the sun, 20
There Will Come a Time, 167
There will come a time, lovely creature, 167
They lasted longer then, 75
They look pinched by a wind, 174
They're not touching, 40
This cake I'm making, 162
This could be the still centre, 55
This frail-looking balustrade, 191
This is the season when the myth-makers, 117
This is the world's third hottest place, 46
This is where we sat, 87
This Morning, 143
*This painting proceeds like the drunkard's
    walk: reversible, and slow*, 34
This ship is full of empty passengers, 174
This winter morning, driving north, 65
Those are the worst times, 160
Tide, Turning, 151
To say to the unicorn, 32
Transatlantic, 20
Tuesday at the Office, 180
Turning Point, 176
Twelve, small as six, 81
Two dogs are fighting for your heart, 54
Two old men, 99
Two Quiet Women, 217
Two women, seventies, hold hands, 90

Undine, 218
Upstairs was church, 72

Varanasi, 15
Vertigo, 93
Visiting Duncan, 128
Visiting time. Anna rises from her bed, 122

Waiting, 27
Waiting Room, 144
War Games, 61
War Photographer, 103

Was there one moment when the woman, 164
Watching Swallows, 126
We are the inheritors. We hide here, 138
We brought our mothers' photos in, 111
We dredge these small fry, 140
We form a perfect composition, 114
We have blind spots, 68
We were close once, 135
What shall I say to you, 155
*When, after all those jolts and nearly lost
    connections*, 188
When he asked me that, 121
When I think of her, I see that swift, 152
*When the International Language Crimes
    Tribunal*, 49
When they were young, and she a captive, 129
Where are they now, the women he loved, 13
Where Are You, 157
Where he lives, they get along without them, 170
While his back's turned, I slip inside, 148
Why are we drawn to glass?, 29
Why I Lie in This Place, 134
Wild splashing – a lizard, 53
Wisdom of fools and schoolmasters, 94
Woman Bathing in a Stream: Rembrandt, 113
Woman in Brown, 153
Woman in brown, 153
Woman in Pink, 120
Woman Pursued by Dragon Flees into the
    Desert, 35
Women Walking, 89
Women, stripped to the waist, 118
Words were dustsheets, blinds, 71
Would you have hated it, 15
Wrong-footed, 181

Yellow, 25
*You could spend years of waking hours in
    front of them*, 214
'You did not proper practise', 124
You Make Your Bed, 149
You make your bed, precisely not to lie on it,
    149
You pay for the fifteenth-century palazzo, 179
You tell me about moonstones, 189
You wanted it over, 33
You'd imagined it as a virgin thinks of sex, 47
Young girls up all hours, 115
Your voice silenced by tubes, 79
Yours is the impossible story beyond all stories,
    30
You're going down a long escalator, 181
You're standing in the supermarket queue, 176
You've given me all elements but one, 190
You've put on war paint – dark green stripes,
    61